TH.

Relationship challenges can leave many of us at a loss—how can we fix problems between ourselves and our spouse, within our families, or with other members of the Body of Christ in a way that honors God and affirms the other person? In *The L.O.V.E. Approach*, Peggy Hartshorn gives readers a time-tested, biblically-based tool that can turn difficult relationships around.

—*Jim Daly, President, Focus on the Family*

This gem of a book, written in parable form, makes good on its promise! By diligently using the four steps of *The L.O.V.E Approach*, Peggy Hartshorn offers readers a path that makes relationships happier, restores broken ones, and builds new ones on the solid foundation of trust. Applicable to any situation or setting that involves you and someone else, this tried and true method is transformative! It has blessed me abundantly!

—*Johnnette Benkovic Williams, EWTN Television and Radio Host; Founder and Director, Women of Grace®*

Dr. Peggy's *The L.O.V.E. Approach* is a lifesaver; love never fails.
—*Evangelist Alveda C. King, Civil Rights for the Unborn*

There is literally nobody in the world who does not need what is in this book. Life is about relationships; so is love, freedom, happiness, religion, and salvation. And relationships are about hard work. With wisdom drawn from the Word of God, from her own experience, and from the lives of numerous people who have utilized these steps, my friend and colleague Peggy Hartshorn reveals in *The L.O.V.E. Approach* a concrete path to strengthening relationships and solving problems. This is not just a book that you read. It is a challenge you accept, a journey you embrace, with a commitment to work hard, and to face uncomfortable things you'd rather run away from. But perhaps the biggest challenge is that it's an invitation to hope, that indeed, things do not have to remain as they are. After all, and as God's Word says, LOVE is stronger than death.

—*Fr. Frank Pavone, National Director, Priests for Life*
President, National Pro-life Religious Council

Conversations today too often can divide and polarize us. This is especially tragic within families, ministries, and churches. The issues are tough. How do we solve problems, "share the truth in love," and preserve important relationships? *The L.O.V.E. Approach* provides the answer! Thank you, Peggy Hartshorn, for introducing us to this simple but powerful tool. I highly recommend The L.O.V.E. Approach book to all leaders who want to strengthen relationships and problem solving in their personal and professional lives.

—*The Honorable Bob McEwen, U.S. House of Representatives, Former Member, Ohio*

The beauty of *The L.O.V.E. Approach* is not only that it works so effectively, but that Peggy Hartshorn has modeled this message in her personal and professional life for decades. God has given the Church a real opportunity with this tool to revolutionize the way we meet people at their point of need, help them through their immediate challenge, and see them come out on the other side more aware than ever of His irresistible, unfailing love.

—*John Wootton, Ohio Ministry Network Superintendent, Assemblies of God*

Dr. Peggy Hartshorn's *The L.O.V.E. Approach* is a courageous and compassionate guidebook for all Christians who desperately want to show the love of Jesus to their friends and family. Too many people today have bought the lie that we must compromise God's eternal truth to properly love our neighbors, but Peggy offers a Gospel-centered path forward for believers to hold fast to timeless truth, and boldly live for and share the love of Christ in a hostile culture. Fearless and grace-filled, *The L.O.V.E. Approach* will inspire the young and old to step into a broken world in need of unconditional love.

—*Aaron Baer, President, Citizens for Community Values*

This should be an indispensable resource for students and professionals in human services and health care fields who serve others with a range of life challenges. Readers will learn communication skills to help people to solve their own problems!

—*Martha Shuping, MD, MA, Psychiatrist; President, Ashford Institute for Interdisciplinary Studies*

This book is truly revelatory! Dr. Hartshorn writes compassionately about what she knows personally and professionally—how to L.O.V.E. She provides an illuminating look into how we communicate and effectively shows us ways to do it better. Relevant narratives throughout the book inspire empathy and compel us to see difficult situations differently. Peggy shows us that without The L.O.V.E. Approach, we miss out on the possibility of changing everything.

—*Ryan Bomberger, President, The Radiance Foundation*

What a wonderful book! *The L.O.V.E. Approach* is engaging and impactful, filled with insight and inspiration. It's a must-read for anyone that would like to positively transform their interpersonal relationships with those they "love" and those with whom they may differ.

—*John Murphy, Silicon Valley entrepreneur and Founder/CEO of Active Allies, LLC*

The L.O.V.E. Approach is to relationships what a guided exercise plan is to conditioning, muscle tone, and healthy habits. It is a guided workout plan for the winsome heart—full of instruction, demonstration, and practical exercises. *The Love Approach* will show you how to "bring it" to conflict resolution and crisis intervention. Powerful.

—*Rev. John Ensor, Author; President, PassionLife Ministries*

Pregnancy help medical clinics in Miami have relied on The L.O.V.E. Approach since our founding thirteen years ago. These four simple but powerful steps have helped thousands of women and couples in turmoil find solutions and hope as they face life-and-death choices. I am thrilled that these four steps are now available to the broader Christian community! Couples, families, ministries, small groups, leaders, churches—everyone will now be able to take advantage of the tremendous blessings that come from using The L.O.V.E. Approach!

—*Martha Avila, President, Heartbeat of Miami*

I'm certain The L.O.V.E. Approach will prove to be a vital asset for many ministries striving to help others facing a crisis or struggles in their lives. I highly recommend it!

—*Brad Mattes, President, Life Issues Institute*

Why continue struggling with communication in difficult situations when you can have a highly-effective, step-by-step method to revolutionize your interaction with others: The L.O.V.E. Approach? After reading, you'll wonder how you ever managed without it! I've had Peggy teach The L.O.V.E. Approach to thousands of attendees at events I've organized because it really works!

> —*David Bereit, Founder/Former CEO, 40 Days for Life;*
> *Strategic Advisor, Leadership Mentor*

Dr. Peggy Hartshorn has given the world a treasured gift in her new book, *The L.O.V.E. Approach*. These four simple yet profound steps have been used successfully for decades in the pregnancy help movement, and now families, churches, schools, businesses—literally anyone wanting to build strong relationships and experience authentic connections—can! This book came at the right time for our fractured culture. We need *The L.O.V.E. Approach*!

> —*Carrie Abbott, President, The Legacy Institute*

The Pro-Life Generation can learn a lot from *The L.O.V.E. Approach*. One of our most significant goals is training up this generation to be effective in advancing a culture of life in relationships, at school, at work, and in our society at large. The skills that Peggy teaches for critical thinking and loving decision making will make a difference for this generation as they combine practical problem solving with loving hearts.

> —*Kristan Hawkins, President, Students for Life of America*

Communication is art and craft in the best of circumstances, but even more so when the chips are down: in crisis or loss, where there's anger or fear, when there is resistance even to engage, etc. When we lack method at these times, is it any wonder our outcomes are less than desired? *The L.O.V.E. Approach* is a powerful framework for communication in any situation: family, workplace, and counseling, including those involving significant tension or conflict. And with the use of narrative to illustrate the key tenets, Dr. Hartshorn's book makes the approach easy to absorb and apply. I couldn't recommend this proven model more strongly.

> —*Zeke Swift, Principal, Sage Partnership; Founder,*
> *Southern Africa HIV-AIDS Collaboration*

THE L.O.V.E. APPROACH

4 Proven Steps to Transforming Relationships in Your Family, Church, and Community

Dr. Peggy Hartshorn, PhD

Published by
Heartbeat International Publishing
5000 Arlington Centre Blvd.
Ste. 2277
Columbus, Ohio 43220

Manufactured in the United States of America, or in the United Kingdom when distributed elsewhere.

Hartshorn, Peggy
    The L.O.V.E. Approach: 4 Proven Steps to Transforming
    Relationships in Your Family, Church, and Community
    LCCN: 2020905420
    ISBN: 978-1-951943-10-3
    eBook: 978-1-951943-11-0

Cover design by: Andrea Trudden
Cover photo by: Heartbeat International
Copyediting and interior design: Claudia Volkman
Photo credits: Heartbeat International

Disclaimer: The stories depicted in this book are based on real people and situations known to the author. In all cases, names, identifying information, and particular circumstances have been changed.

TheLOVEApproachBook.com

DEDICATION

The L.O.V.E. Approach book is dedicated to the thousands of volunteers and staff of pregnancy help organizations around the world, in over sixty countries, who have been trained, since 1994, in the four steps—Listen and Learn, Open Options, Vision and Value, and Extend and Empower—through Heartbeat International. You have demonstrated the power of these four steps to build relationships and solve complex problems in a way that honors our Christian values and respects the dignity of each person.

It is also dedicated to all who have recognized that The L.O.V.E. Approach can be used in almost all situations where relationships are important and crucial issues need to be resolved, especially to my creative friend and colleague Betty McDowell, in particular, who gently prodded me to write this book and who suggested the form of a fable. In following this challenge, I tried to write an "engaging" story that, with God's grace, can bring understanding, healing, and unity to our most important relationships in these challenging times.

TABLE OF CONTENTS

Introduction...ix

Chapter 1: Class One, The L.O.V.E. Approach.................1

Chapter 2: Tools for The L.O.V.E. Approach.................11

Chapter 3: Class Two, The L Step, Listen and Learn 21

Chapter 4: Tools for the L Step.................37

Chapter 5: Michael Tries the L Step.................51

Chapter 6: Class Three, The O Step, Open Options.................57

Chapter 7: Tools for the O Step.................71

Chapter 8: Mariana Tries the O Step.................81

Chapter 9: Class Four, The V Step, Vision and Value.................89

Chapter 10: Tools for the V Step.................101

Chapter 11: Katy Tries the V Step.................107

Chapter 12: Class Five, The E Step, Extend and Empower.........115

Chapter 13: Tools for the E Step.................129

Chapter 14: Josh Tries the E Step.................133

Chapter 15: Reunion: Michael, Mariana, Katy, and Josh Meet Again....141

Acknowledgments.................145

INTRODUCTION

This book, written in an easy-to-read story form, answers the questions "What can I say or do when communicating with a person I care about who is angry, withdrawn, hopeless, in crisis, confused, or obstinate? How can I help clarify and even resolve issues and problems in a way that preserves relationships and is consistent with my deepest values as a Christian?"

I'll introduce you to four steps—L (Listen and Learn), O (Open Options), V (Vision and Value), and E (Extend and Empower)—that can be transformational, especially when used between husbands and wives, within families, and within church communities. Using these four steps, ordinary Christians who interact with each other at home, in the community, and in church settings can bring hope and solutions to problems that before seemed daunting.

While The L.O.V.E. Approach is based on 1 Corinthians 13:1-8: "Love is patient, love is kind, . . . it is not arrogant or rude . . . love does not insist on its own way," this book is not didactic, nor is it denominational or theological.

Instead, it's written for people of good will who try to follow the Golden Rule and who bring those good intentions into relationship building and problem solving.

In the following pages, you'll meet four strangers who come

together in a training class offered by a group of churches and faith-based groups. Each of the four is facing a critical problem or relationship issue: Michael as a spouse, Mariana as a church administrator, Katy as a ministry volunteer, and Josh as a parent.

The story follows these four as they open up to each other, try The L.O.V.E. Approach with the people they care about, and reunite later to share how their situations and relationships have been transformed.

The narrative is based on real people and situations known to the author, but the names and the details have been changed to protect confidentiality.

How to Use This Book

Narrative chapters demonstrate the foundational basis for The L.O.V.E. Approach and how to use each step—L (Listen and Learn), O (Open Options), V (Vision and Value), and E (Extend and Empower)—and show each of the characters using the steps in a real-life situation.

These chapters are interspersed with others that offer practice for each step, including space for personal reflection and questions and answers.

You can read and practice on your own, but it's even better to have one or more partners working with you so you can share your responses and learn from each other, just as Michael, Mariana, Katy, and Josh do in the narrative chapters.

This book is a perfect resource for individuals, couples, family members, friends, leaders, teams, small groups, ministries, and churches. It can be used, for example, by one couple or within a family, in informal book clubs, couples' support groups, small group ministries, women's or men's groups, home-based ministries, and study groups, or as the text for evening retreat sessions or weekend retreats (for couples, families, or church staffs and ministry teams). It can be the basis of a training in The L.O.V.E. Approach for any church or faith-based organization.

Personal Note from the Author

In 1994, I developed The L.O.V.E. Approach to explain how Christ-centered pregnancy help volunteers can build relationships with women facing difficult pregnancies and help them resolve issues and problems in a life-affirming way. It has been in continuous use around the world, taught by Heartbeat International since then (person to person and now online).

It was originally inspired by the lessons I learned the hard way from painful experience as a young wife, mother, friend, teacher, and passionate Christian volunteer and leader over forty years ago. Now I offer the four steps to you and the larger Christian community in the expectation that you will also find them powerful in your own relationships and ministries.

God bless you as you learn The L.O.V.E. Approach and put it to life-changing work in your life and with those you care about!

CHAPTER 1

───◆───

CLASS ONE—THE L.O.V.E. APPROACH

As they mingled with the larger group and took seats in the church hall, four of the new trainees were unaware that their stories were about to intersect, with dramatic results, and that they would only know the full extent of the impact six months from that very evening.

The four—two men and two women of different ages, ethnic groups, backgrounds, personalities, and experiences—had deep common needs, as they would soon discover.

But only one commonality was obvious at that point—they had landed next to each other on the first evening of the bi-monthly training course in The L.O.V.E. Approach offered by the Christian Coalition. The class was required, or strongly recommended, by nearly every church and faith-based organization in their community for all employees and volunteers. Over one hundred students were starting this class, and they hailed from forty different churches and organizations.

As they waited for the class to begin, Michael Harmon, a highly analytical accountant, was thinking about the frosty good-bye from his young wife. Their marriage, he was reluctantly

1

concluding, was a big mistake. His new position on the board of the St. John Food Pantry would at least get him out of the uncomfortable atmosphere in his home.

Josh Jefferson, a top sales executive who was never at a loss for words, was talking in a hushed tone to someone on his cell. The call ended abruptly, and Josh had a perplexed look on his face as he stared at the phone in his hand. Surely volunteering at the King Ranch with fatherless boys would be easier than dealing with his own son at this point.

Katy Klein, a sensitive mother of four, was re-experiencing some of the same sense of helplessness that she felt when she started facilitating the small group for women at her church. It was the pain on the women's faces when they told their stories the first night—past abuse, broken relationships, pregnancy loss. She had just started working in this ministry in her parish, but she was already thinking of giving up. Could this course she was required to take help?

Mariana Delgado, newly hired administrator for one of the community's mega churches, was on her tablet, finishing notes on one of the church employees. Her stomach was churning. She couldn't allow missed goals—or his insubordination. With many years of administrative experience under her belt in the corporate world, she knew how to apply business principles to get the church staff into shape, but the resistance was more than she anticipated.

The four were immersed in their worries as the first speaker came to the podium.

"Welcome. I'm Dr. Alex Meyer, executive director of Community Social Services, one of the member groups of our Christian Coalition. I'm so glad you're all here to learn The L.O.V.E. Approach—a crucial tool for relationship building and problem solving. I know I speak for all Coalition member groups and churches that require this training for everyone involved in leadership and ministry. We are confident that, by learning and modeling this approach, we will see it being used more and more, not only in our churches and faith-based organizations, but also in our homes and communities—with life-giving and life-changing results!

"I'm a champion of The L.O.V.E. Approach! It's changed my personal life. If it weren't for a Christian brother who knew The L.O.V.E. Approach and used it with me when I was in a crisis, I wouldn't be here with you tonight. And my wife, Sharon, says we wouldn't be married for twenty years if it weren't for The L.O.V.E. Approach! But that's my personal story. I'll share more of it with you as we continue to meet."

There was a general murmur. Dr. Meyer's comment had piqued the interest of Michael, Josh, Mariana, Katy, along with most of the others in the room.

"But before I turn the session over to our trainer, I'll call on my colleague Bishop Isaiah Wilson of Victory Bible Church to open our training in prayer."

"Lord," intoned the Bishop slowly and deeply, "thank You for equipping us to love each other more through The L.O.V.E. Approach that we will be learning. Thank You for how it has helped me do my job—to counsel the brothers and sisters in my congregation and bring them closer to You. Open our hearts and minds, and especially our ears today. You gave us two ears and only one mouth, and we need to use them in that proportion. Amen?"

After a lukewarm "Amen" from the room, Bishop Wilson tried again, a little more loudly.

"Maybe your ears aren't open yet? . . . Amen?"

Smiles and a rousing "Amen" came from the group. Everyone now seemed focused on what promised to be an intriguing evening.

"Now," continued Dr. Meyer, "it's my pleasure to introduce our trainer, Mary Elizabeth McDowell, the founder of Guadalupe Center, who has had many years of experience teaching The L.O.V.E. Approach."

Mary Elizabeth stood up to polite applause and came to the podium.

"Thank you," she said confidently and warmly. "I'll be with you during these five classes to teach you the process that I predict will be life-changing for you — and for those you share it with. Let's get right to it."

She clicked on and read the first Power Point slide:

The L.O.V.E. Approach:
Four Steps To Transforming Relationships
and Problem Solving

"We call this 'The L.O.V.E. Approach' for several reasons. First, it is a loving, caring, nonjudgmental way of building trust and respect and of entering into relationship-based problem solving.

"The behavior we try to model in order to do this is described in Paul's first letter to the Corinthians, chapter 13, verses 1–8."

She clicked to the next slide and read each line clearly as it scrolled slowly onto the screen:

And I show you a still more excellent way.

If I speak in the tongues of men and of angels, but do not have love, I am a noisy gong or a clanging cymbal.

If I have prophetic powers, and understand all mysteries

and all knowledge; and if I have all faith, so as to remove mountains, but have not love, I am nothing.

And if I give away all I have, and if I deliver my body to be burned, but have not love, I gain nothing.

Love is patient and kind, love is not jealous or boastful, it is not arrogant or rude. Love does not insist on its own way, it is not irritable or resentful, it does not rejoice at wrong, but rejoices in the right. Love bears all things, believes all things, hopes all things, endures all things.

Love never ends.

Mary Elizabeth observed a wide range of facial expressions, from quizzical to somber, as the words sank in.

Then she offered this encouragement: "Human nature being what it is, this kind of behavior does not come naturally, especially when we are under stress or faced with a difficult situation or even with a difficult person."

Josh glanced at Michael, sitting next to him, and whispered, "My son."

Michael responded, "My wife." They exchanged a look of mutual understanding.

"As Christians," noted Mary Elizabeth, "we know that God is love. All love comes from God, and the closer we are to Him, the more His love flows through us, and the more we can act like Him, and the more we can speak the truth in love."

Mariana glanced at the sweet face of Katy beside her. "I have lots of trouble with that kind of speaking, but I bet you don't," she whispered.

Katy whispered back, "Most of the time, I don't know what to speak at all."

The class, following instructions, opened their training notebooks to the section "What About Me?" They started jotting down their reflections on the first question:

> What one or two ideas or lines from Paul's Letter to the Corinthians speak to me about either a behavior I need to avoid or a behavior I want to model in my relationship with others?

Mary Elizabeth finally invited the group to break into pairs and share something from their writing with a partner. People started to move around, quietly at first, and then the room began buzzing.

Josh and Michael shook hands, after moving their chairs to face each other. Michael looked pensive.

Josh spoke up right away. "Hey, it's obvious! The line that jumps out at me is 'Love is patient and kind.' Usually, that's not me. I can sell just about anything to anybody. I'm not real humble either, I guess. I mean, I usually have all the answers. So I don't have much patience when people have problems."

Michael responded. "I hate to admit it, but the line that hits me is if 'I understand all mysteries and all knowledge, but have not love, I am nothing.' I wrote this down: 'I always want more information and facts. I'm really good at getting to the bottom line, then telling people what I think, but it probably seems to them that I don't care.'"

Mariana and Katy had moved their chairs closer. Mariana confessed, "I relate to the part that says 'If I have all faith, so as to remove mountains, but do not have love, I am nothing.' I've been told that I can be like a bulldozer. Not even a mountain seems like an obstacle. But I keep forgetting I'm dealing with real people. I tend to move too fast. I probably sound like a noisy gong to them."

Katy seemed amazed. "I'm almost the opposite, I guess. I feel powerless. I don't want to be involved with people when their problems are so complex. Sometimes I give up and withdraw. This line convicts me: 'Love bears all things, believes all things, hopes all things, endures all things. Love never ends.'"

Mary Elizabeth moved around the room, catching bits and pieces of the sharing.

Calling the group back together, she summarized the powerful admissions. "It sounds as though you all are realizing that your own behavior can be more loving, but I bet you're also wondering, *Is that really doable?* Let me assure you that it is possible—especially through a closer relationship to God, who IS love. When we are filled up, we can pour out."

"And, even when you don't feel loving or very close to God," she added, "you can still speak or respond to another person in a way that says 'I care about you and the issue you (or we) are facing.'"

"We call that a decision to love. Love is an act of the will and will lead to loving behavior."

Noticing some quizzical looks from the trainees, Mary Elizabeth continued, "When we decide to behave in a loving manner, even if we don't feel loving, that can change our feelings too, and it certainly changes relationships. Sometimes we might also need to make a decision to accept love, even if we don't feel particularly lovable. We are called to both give and to receive love. We'll talk more tomorrow night about how our thoughts and feelings are related, and I hope this will all become clearer!

"Now, it's time for a break. Perhaps get a bit of fresh air, and let's come back together in fifteen minutes."

———————

Mary Elizabeth stepped back to the podium with an encouraging smile. "Tonight we're going lay the groundwork for the four steps of The L.O.V.E. Approach, looking at ourselves and any barriers we put up to real communication and problem solving. We all have habits that are *not* the kinds of loving behaviors described in Paul's Letter to the Corinthians!

"Too often those habits really say, I don't care about you, or I don't have time for you, or even, I don't agree with you from the start, so why are we even talking about this?"

There was visible discomfort in the room as the trainees started reading the slide that Mary Elizabeth put up on the screen:

10 Barriers to Listening

1. Being Distracted
2. Thinking of My Answer
3. Interrupting
4. Pacifying
5. Lightening Up or Joking
6. Focusing on Facts
7. Finishing Sentences
8. Defending Myself
9. Judging
10. Sympathizing, not Empathizing

"Now, turn to "What About Me?" in your notebooks and spend some time working through the materials, including the

Barriers and the section on body language and tone of voice. When you're finished, share with your partner what you're learning about your own communication habits." Mary Elizabeth added, with a smile and a wink, "For better or for worse!"

The class dutifully started jotting down responses in their notebooks. When it was time to share, Josh and Michael looked at each other sheepishly.

Josh began. "No question . . . when I looked at the list of bad habits, I checked nearly every one! My worst is being distracted—reaching for my cell, even texting when someone is talking to me. When my son talks, he's all over the place—but I am too. So, I finish his sentences, make a joke so nothing gets too long or serious. I'm thinking of something else, too—my tone shows it," Josh admitted. "No wonder he hung up on me tonight," he added.

Michael decided he could confide in Josh. "I'll be honest," he said, "my wife tells me I'm all facts, that all I want to do is get the information, solve the problem, and move on. She says I don't care about her feelings. She's pointed out my body language too—crossed arms, no real eye contact. I'm not proud of it. I checked off lots of the bad habits. You're not alone!"

Katy and Mariana were sitting close, eye to eye.

Katy started. "It's good to have someone to share this with. I think the biggest thing for me, especially when someone has a problem . . . my heart goes out to them and I get bogged down in sympathy, in feeling sorry for them. I want everyone to be at peace, but the situations are too complicated, and I can't solve the problems. I feel helpless, so I close down and withdraw."

Mariana responded, "Opposites attract! I really don't even empathize when someone comes to me with a problem, especially at work. I interrupt, hurry them along, usually thinking, *I've heard all this before.* I'm judging that they aren't very smart. I'm goal-oriented, with lots of things to do. I'm sure my body language says I don't have time for what they're saying—and I don't. But I'm not proud of that."

As the various pairs continued sharing, Mary Elizabeth could see relationships forming among the trainees. There was good eye contact between partners; people were leaning in toward each other, and that encouraged more intimate sharing. She knew they would need the growing level of trust with their partners for what she would ask them to do the following evening.

But it was time to interrupt. "I hate to break up such honest discussions, but our time tonight is coming to a close. In moving around the room, I hear most of you saying that you recognize your behaviors that are indeed barriers to good communication—and you're open to learning more. Great!

"Be ready when we meet again to delve more deeply into The L.O.V.E. Approach. As we saw tonight, it's based on loving behavior, hence the name.

"But it's also called The L.O.V.E. Approach because of its four practical steps, which we will start learning tomorrow night," Mary Elizabeth said as she clicked on the next slide.

> **L** = Listen and Learn
> **O** = Open Options
> **V** = Vision and Value
> **E** = Extend and Empower

CHAPTER 2

—⇒●⇐—

TOOLS FOR THE L.O.V.E. APPROACH

So faith, hope, love abide, these three;
but the greatest of these is love.

1 CORINTHIANS 13:13

The best way to work through the practice exercises in this book is to have a partner or a small group of people who agree to work together. After privately writing your answers, you share your answers with your partner or small group—or both.

You can do the practice exercises on your own, but, when you share your answers with at least one other person, you get more ideas and encouragement, and you'll move forward more quickly in learning and successfully using The L.O.V.E. Approach.

Before you learn more about the four practical steps of The L.O.V.E. Approach, it's important to reflect, like Michael, Josh, Mariana, and Katy, on the basis for this approach, 1 Corinthians 13:1–8, which describes true loving behavior.

Because God is love, it's also important to take stock of your relationship with Him. Love comes from Him, into us, and then through us to other people. Examining your past communication behaviors and reflecting on your body language and tone of voice are also helpful.

WHAT ABOUT ME?

Remember, the behavior we try to model is like the behavior Paul described in 1 Corinthians 13:1–8.

> And I show you a still more excellent way.
> If I speak in the tongues of men and of angels, but do not have love, I am a noisy gong or a clanging cymbal.
> If I have prophetic powers, and understand all mysteries and all knowledge; and if I have all faith, so as to remove mountains, but have not love, I am nothing.
> And if I give away all I have, and if I deliver my body to be burned, but have not love, I gain nothing.
> Love is patient and kind, love is not jealous or boastful, it is not arrogant or rude. Love does not insist on its own way, it is not irritable or resentful, it does not rejoice at wrong, but rejoices in the right. Love bears all things, believes all things, hopes all things, endures all things.
> Love never ends.

What one or two ideas or lines from Paul's First Letter to the Corinthians speak to me about either a behavior I need to avoid or a behavior I want to model in my relationship with others?

What is my relationship with the Lord, the source of love, right now? Do I feel filled up with His love so that it flows out of me to others? How do I feel about my answer?

If I want to be more filled up with the love of God, what steps or actions could I take to move in this direction? (If you cannot think of any steps here and you are working through these exercises without a partner or small group to help you, be sure to ask for help on answering this question, right now, from your pastor or another wise advisor.)

PRACTICE

Put a check in front of any (or all!) of the ten behaviors that describe a habit of yours that may actually be a barrier to loving communication. Then, underneath the behavior, indicate a specific person or situation where this behavior is or could seem unloving to another person (spouse, child, sibling, friend, co-worker, boss, subordinate, colleague in the community, neighbor, person in your church, etc.).

These behaviors are often interpreted (rightly or wrongly) as "I am not focusing on you," and sometimes they even say "I don't really care about you." They are barriers to relationship building and problem solving.

1.____ Being distracted while the other person is talking (using my smartphone, texting, watching TV, glancing at the time, thinking about what I have to do next, multitasking, etc.).

2.____ Thinking about what I will say next (my answer, my solution, my alternative, etc.).

3.____ Interrupting, rather than being silent or waiting for the person to finish.

4.____ Pacifying right away instead of focusing on the person or problem as he or she talks ("Don't worry," "Things will look better tomorrow," "Calm down," "Just turn it over to the Lord").

5.____ Using humor, kidding, or joking to deflect the problem or negative feelings.

6.____ Focusing almost solely on facts or details as you listen (so you can provide information or solve the problem).

7.____ Jumping to conclusions or finishing sentences ("I've heard all this before," "He has it all wrong").

8.____ Being defensive as you listen ("If he/she had only done what I suggested," "This is not my fault").

9.____ Making negative judgments about the person sharing ("I don't like the way she looks or talks," "He's not very smart, articulate, well-behaved," "People from that group always have trouble with . . .").

10.____ Sympathizing ("I pity/feel sorry for people who have to deal with X") instead of empathizing ("I can almost feel the anger/loneliness/happiness she is expressing").

REFLECTION
(Share your answers with your partner or small group)

What are the two or three most important behaviors I need to work on so other people know that I am really focusing on them and what they are sharing?

Is there a situation recently where I consciously made a decision to love? Did I do something loving, even though I did not feel loving? Is there a situation recently where I could have done something loving but did not and now I regret that? Is there a situation recently where someone made a decision to do something loving for me, but I did not accept that love and now I regret that?

PRACTICE

Body language actually is more accurate in conveying a message than verbal language! Your body language should convey to the other person that you are ready and willing to listen. The acronym SOLER helps us remember what body language signals "I am focusing on you." Of course, the opposite body language indicates the opposite message.

S—Sit squarely. Sit directly facing the person to whom you want to listen.

O—Open posture. By not having your arms or legs crossed, you signal that you are nonjudgmental and not defensive.

L—Lean. You "lean into" or move closer to the person you want to listen to, without getting into his or her private space.

E—Eye contact. Generally, to show you are open to listening, you look directly into the eyes of the person who is talking; however, in some cultures, looking directly into a person's eyes is considered disrespectful.

R—Relaxed posture. Your body should not be tense or rigid.

Tone of voice is also crucial in listening. Your tone of voice needs to be caring and loving to encourage other people to share more fully with you. (Remember how 1 Corinthians 13 describes the "noisy gong" and "clanging cymbal"!)

In addition, be sure that the person you want to listen to is comfortable. Lack of comfort is indicated by a rigid position, crossed arms or legs, poor eye contact.

If the other person has suffered trauma in the past, he or she may be tempted to revert to a fight, flight, or freeze response when you are trying to provide help and support. Try to put the other person at ease by offering a more comfortable chair or something to drink before you begin to listen.

REFLECTION
(Share your answers with your partner or small group)

When I am conversing with another person, am I conscious of my own body language?

Do I notice the body language of the other person?

Give an example from a conversation you remember, if possible. Is this something you want to work on?

Is it natural or unnatural for me to use a caring and loving voice when I am discussing an issue or problem with another person? Why or why not?

Give an example from a conversation you remember, if possible. Is this something you want to work on?

CHAPTER 3

CLASS TWO—THE L STEP
LISTEN AND LEARN

As the trainees gathered again the next evening, it was clear that relationships had begun to form; people were beginning to be vulnerable with their partners. After some initial chatter as they took their seats, the trainees focused their attention on the first slide, already on the screen:

L = **Listen and Learn**
O = Open Options
V = Vision and Value
E = Extend and Empower

Mary Elizabeth began with a reminder. "If we come to our conversations with a decision to love—a loving attitude and intention, as we discussed in our first class—we can use these four practical steps to transform relationships and solve problems in almost any situation.

"Listen and Learn is the foundational step, so we'll spend more time practicing that than on all the other three steps put together.

"Listen and Learn is also the most difficult step since we

must let the other person do almost all of the talking. That's especially hard if words seem to roll easily off your tongue, or if solutions come quickly to your mind, or if it seems like you've heard all this before."

A look of self-recognition quickly passed over Mariana's face. Josh nudged Michael and whispered, "That's me. We're men; we solve problems, right?"

"Instead of offering options or solutions (the O step), providing a new vision (the V step), or extending help with a practical plan (the E Step), you may just have to bite your tongue in the L step," Mary Elizabeth continued.

There were chuckles from many in the room.

"The three magic words in the L step are 'Tell me more . . .'

"If the person is having trouble sharing or opening up (even when you simply say, 'Tell me more'), we have a series of tools called the Listening and Learning Wheels that will remind you of what areas you can explore and what questions you can ask to help draw that person out. The first of these wheels is called the Self Wheel," Mary Elizabeth said, clicking on the next slide.

SELF WHEEL

"As the listener, you can help the other person share his or her **Feelings, Thoughts, Wants, Values,** and **Beliefs**, as you see on the Self Wheel. Besides saying 'Tell me more . . .,' you can ask simple questions based on these areas of self-awareness, such as:

'How does that make you feel?'
'What did you think then?'
'What would you want to do, if it were an option?'
'Does that relate to what you value most now or to your deepest beliefs?'

"If you are trying to help another person resolve an issue or problem, or even simply build a deeper relationship, helping that person explore all of these areas is key.

"In fact, sometimes the other person will verbalize a great solution—will jump to the O step—without your having to do much more than really listen as they express their thoughts, feelings, wants, values, and beliefs! This is an art that can be learned, and we're going to practice it," Mary Elizabeth said with an encouraging smile as she clicked to the next slide.

Pointers for Using the Self Wheel

- **Feelings** are physical. For example, a quicker heartbeat may accompany a feeling of fear or anxiety.
- **Feelings** and **Thoughts** are sometimes confused. "I feel that . . ." is really a **Thought**, not a **Feeling**.
- **Feelings** are neither right nor wrong, but an action based on feelings may be right or wrong.
- **Thoughts** and **Beliefs** may be correct or incorrect, and sometimes they need clarification.

- **Feelings** influence **Thoughts, Beliefs,** and **Wants,** and **Thoughts, Beliefs,** and **Wants** influence **Feelings.**
- **Values** and **Beliefs** (what we hold most dear) are often not easily expressed.
- **Wants** may be the area most difficult to share (it makes us most vulnerable, especially in personal relationships).

Michael and Mariana were busily taking notes and trying to absorb all the interesting new information.

Katy was feeling a little fearful and overwhelmed by it all.

Josh's hand sprang up. "Even if I ask the best questions to understand all these areas, what am I getting at? I mean, I think I missed the 'why.'"

"Thank you, Josh," Mary Elizabeth said, laughing. "Sometimes asking a person point-blank 'Why?' can be intimidating, so I don't recommend that question when you are listening.

"But I'm teaching, not sharing my deepest self, so you are not putting me on the spot if you ask me why! Here's my answer: First, a person feels valued when you allow that person to fully tell his or her own story—without the barriers that we discussed in our first class. So, listening alone is a loving act.

"Second, listening builds the relationship. It builds trust. When it is your turn to talk (in the O, V, and E steps), the person will be more likely to listen to you—and that's crucial, especially if the issue to be resolved is between the two of you or if you have the resources to help resolve a problem the other person is facing.

"The third reason we explore all these areas of self-awareness is to get a fuller picture of who the other person is, inside and outside. What I mean is that when a person shares feelings, thoughts, and other areas of self-awareness related to the issue or problem, his or her resources and needs also become clearer.

"The more we know about the other person, the better we can discuss all the possible options, share vision, and extend and empower.

"This slide clarifies the process, I hope! I like to think of listening and learning as 'turning the wheels' to reveal different sides of the issue, all of the person's areas of self-awareness, resources, and needs. Then we can move forward in the most informed way."

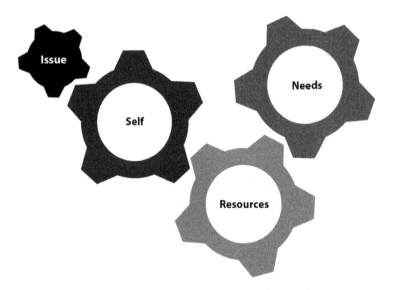

LISTENING AND LEARNING WHEELS

"For example, let's say the issue is that you are the caregiver for your aging mother just diagnosed with dementia. In the self wheel, you are aware of your feelings of sadness, anxiety, and uncertainty, you think most options will be impossible financially, and you want to provide the most appropriate care because you value your mother so much.

"In the needs wheel, you realize that you need a lot more information, probably financial help, and emotional support. But, in the resources wheel, you soon discover there are specialists in your community, support groups, lots of community referrals, even a prayer line. As you explore each wheel, one turns the other, changing your perspective. Things begin to look different. Your feelings now include hope, and your needs don't seem as great because you see resources to address them. The issue itself begins to look different to you."

After Mary Elizabeth explained the slide and the relationship between the issue and the wheels, she paused for a moment to let the students absorb the more complex diagram. Then she announced: "I want to reintroduce Dr. Alex Meyer, the executive director of Community Social Services and coordinator of the Christian Coalition."

"Hello again," said Dr. Meyer with a warm smile. "I told you I'd be back to tell the story of how The L.O.V.E. Approach changed my life. One way to understand the value of the Listening and Learning Wheels is to hear a personal story of how they work.

"I was on the receiving end, listened to by someone who had been trained in using the wheels. That was fifteen years ago, but I'll never forget it. I ran into my old high school coach outside a sporting goods store. Our talk changed the trajectory of my life. That's why I make sure we teach the wheels to everyone we can.

"When Coach asked how I was doing, I said, 'Great,' but my

face must have revealed the truth. Coach asked if I had some time to catch up, and when I said yes, he suggested the coffee shop next door. When we were face-to-face, he put his phone on mute, looked me straight in the eye, and said quietly, 'Tell me what's going on.'

"I blurted out that my dream job, a career as a personal counselor, had turned into a nightmare.

"He asked me to tell him more about it . . . starting with what was going through my head. I told him I thought all the time and money spent on my years of education had been a waste. To be fair to everyone, I thought I should quit. I was getting dragged into problems and getting angry with the very people I wanted to help. I didn't think I was making enough money to be the family provider that I had always wanted to be. My wife complained that I was never home, that all I cared about was my clients. We didn't talk much anymore.

"When he asked me about my feelings, I admitted that I felt lonely, burned out, exhausted, dry, discouraged. I believed God had called me into this, and now He had let me down.

"My old coach didn't say much. He just kept asking me to tell him more. Because of his encouragement—I could hear it in his tone of voice and see it in his eyes—I kept sharing. He didn't interrupt, except to ask for clarifications to make sure he really got my story.

"It seemed like he listened to me for an hour—it felt so good to get it all out—but I later realized it was only about fifteen minutes!

"I now see that he was listening not only for my areas of self-awareness, but also listening for my resources and needs—like you see on the Listening and Learning Wheels. And we were

27

turning those wheels around as we examined the issue—my nightmare job.

"When Coach started talking, he told me that he could see I had lots of resources: my years of education and skills, my passion for helping people. He said my story showed that I was determined, a hard worker, and trying to follow God's direction for my life. He said he also heard some big needs: I was getting pulled into the crises of my counseling clients and didn't know what to do about it. He heard me say that I didn't feel emotionally supported by my wife, but that I hadn't really been able to discuss much personally with her. Our income was so tight that I couldn't quit my job, and my relationship with God was distant. He said that he sensed my feeling of being trapped and even abandoned.

"He nailed it. When the look on my face confirmed it, he told me that he was here to help, and that together we could explore my options and develop a plan. He told me I was not alone.

"I remember him asking, 'Are you willing to talk through options with me?' And I remember saying, 'Please!' It had been pretty emotional for me to open up so much. We both knew I needed time to regroup! We agreed on a time and place to sit down again and think through my options together. Our handshake on leaving the coffee shop left me with a sense of hope.

"I'll be back again tomorrow night to tell you about how Coach took me through the O step. Tonight, I just want you to know that he loved me through my crisis, beginning with listening and learning from his heart."

As Dr. Meyer left the podium, the room was quiet. The trainees were deep in thought.

Michael's mind turned to Dr. Meyer's mention of his distant

relationship with his wife. He must have eventually shared his feelings with her too, thought Michael. That must have been hard.

Mariana wondered if she could ever do that kind of coaching with the employees she dealt with. It was a vision that inspired her.

Katy related to feeling discouraged and overwhelmed with the problems of people she encountered in ministry. Perhaps there was hope for her.

Josh was wondering if he could ever be such a great listener, especially when it came to his son. His thoughts were interrupted by Mary Elizabeth, bringing them all back to the present.

"I hope Dr. Meyer's story gives you an example of how a caring person can use the Listening and Learning Wheels to help someone in the L step. That can lead to really tackling an issue or problem using the other steps of The L.O.V.E. Approach. You can do it, too, with a little practice!"

Mary Elizabeth instructed them to turn to their training notebooks. "Open to the practice on the Listening and Learning Wheels. When you see that you and your partner are finished, get back into your teams and share your answers."

The trainees worked quickly through the practice exercises on their own. Then they shared easily as they helped one another distinguish different areas of self-awareness and learn how to delve more deeply into a particular thought or feeling, recognizing resources and needs.

Mary Elizabeth called them back together. "You've worked hard and it's time for a break," she told the trainees. "But when we get back, I have something for you that I promise will take your learning to an entirely deeper level. It's my favorite part of our training, so don't go away!"

———————

When the class returned after the break, they seemed refreshed and ready to take their listening and learning lesson to some deeper level—whatever Mary Elizabeth meant!

"We're now going to actually practice listening and learning with each other," said their trainer. "I'd like each team of two to find another team of two close by and arrange your chairs in a circle."

It was the first time Katy and Mariana had spoken to Michael and Josh, although the four had been sitting next to one another since the training began. It was also the first time their four stories would intersect, but not the last.

They shook hands and exchanged pleasantries.

"Now," Mary Elizabeth interrupted, "I want each of you to think of an issue or problem that you are currently facing, one that you are willing to share at a somewhat personal level with at least one other person in your group. It could be something like what to do in the care of an elderly parent or how to deal with a difficult situation on the job or with a neighbor or family member. When you have an issue, raise your hand."

She waited until all hands were raised. "Now I want you to turn to the person you have paired up with during the class so far. First, one of you will be the listener. The other person will be the sharer, telling your partner about the issue you have identified. When I say time is up, reverse. The person who was the listener will be the sharer and vice versa.

"When you are the listener, remember that the other person should be doing most of the talking. Your job is to help the person share his or her feelings, thoughts, wants, values, and beliefs by asking good questions and inviting the person to share more, using good body language and a loving tone, like we discussed in the first class. You will also be learning about the person's resources and needs.

"Focus only on the L step. You don't want to jump into solving the problem, giving solutions, providing advice, or offering a new vision. Just listen!

"Now, quickly share the issue with your partner—in just one or two sentences before we begin."

Katy looked at Mariana and confided, "I don't know what to do about leading my weekly women's ministry group. I'm overwhelmed with the problems these sisters in faith bring up. I'm not a professional counselor. I'm a full-time mom. Maybe I should just quit, but I'm not at peace with that either."

Mariana shared, "I have an issue with a church employee who is underperforming and not following directives. No matter what I say when I meet with him, our meetings always end in frustration, and nothing changes."

Michael leaned in toward Josh. "I have to say, my problem is very personal. Every conversation with my wife ends with her saying that I just don't understand—and me not knowing what else to say. We are at a stalemate."

Josh confided, "Well, mine is personal too. It's my son. He's not the kid anymore who wants to be with Dad. In fact, I think there is something big happening, but he won't let me in on it."

The four, along with the rest of the class, seemed a little uncomfortable. There were concerned looks on some faces.

Quickly, the trainees faced each other in pairs, and Mary Elizabeth gave the instructions. The sharer was to share, and the listener was to listen.

The room reverberated with noise, sounding almost chaotic,

as the many pairs of men and women began communicating earnestly.

Mary Elizabeth walked around slowly, smiling as she noted people gesturing with their hands, leaning into one other for more intimacy, and changing facial expressions and tone of voice. The volume increased and then decreased in waves as the sharing continued.

This activity was her favorite part of the training. It always generated such energy in the room as participants began using new skills.

It was evident that they were learning—making breakthroughs in their ability to listen as well as to share. She noticed smiles on some faces and concentration lines on others. Occasionally, one person reached out his hand to the other or someone offered a tissue to her partner.

In each pair, one person was sharing earnestly and the other was intently listening, asking good questions, urging his or her partner to share more through effective body language and eye contact. The pairs were engaged.

Reluctantly, she had to disrupt the groups after only about five minutes. It was time for the sharers to become the listeners.

The pairs changed roles, and Mary Elizabeth watched with satisfaction as the room came alive with sharing and listening again.

Finally, Mary Elizabeth called the room to order, with some difficulty, to tell the trainees it was time to end their sharing in pairs and move into their circles of four.

"I hate to break up such great use of the L step," announced Mary Elizabeth, raising her voice to be heard over the conversations that were winding down. "But I want you to share now, in your circle of four, what you have learned by this exercise and what it has meant to you. Our class is almost at an end this evening, but please make time for everyone to share. Here is a slide with the questions I want your group to discuss."

When you were the Sharer . . .
- How did you feel being listened to?
- What did your listener say or do to help you share more fully?
- How did the experience of being listened to influence where you are in the process of dealing with your issue or solving your problem?

When you were the Listener . . .
- How did it feel to be the listener?
- Was it difficult for you to just listen and not get into the problem-solving steps (O,V,E)?

Did you develop a relationship during the L Step? Why or why not?

As the trainees glanced up at the questions, they quickly began to talk again, this time in their small groups.

Our four, now sitting in a circle, had each been through the powerful experience of being listened to intently from the heart. They were eager to share with one another their own experience. They also wanted to tell what it had been like to be the listener, trying so hard not to interrupt their partners or offer solutions to the problems. They patiently waited for their turns, going around the circle one by one, starting with Mariana, then Katy, Josh, and finally Michael.

It was somewhat exhausting, but also powerful and bonding,

to hear how each one felt being listened to and being the listener.

Perhaps because he was the last one to share, and because he wanted to act on his experience immediately, Michael's sharing made the biggest impact on the four.

"When I was the sharer, Josh really did a great job drawing me out—I didn't have much to say at first, or I didn't want to get into something so personal, but Josh had been the sharer first and he told me all about his relationship with his son. The trust he showed in me gave me the courage, I guess, to share with him when it was my turn.

"He was patient and quiet—he didn't put me on the spot with hard questions. Finally, I told him how I felt about my marriage—disappointed, and disappointed in myself. I'm not a good husband—like I always wanted to be—since I really don't understand my wife. I don't know how to show her that I care—which I do!

"I realized tonight that I don't listen to her—not in the way we're learning. I never share what's really going on inside of me at all, at least not my feelings or wants. I'm full of thoughts and ideas, whenever she can even get my attention!

"I never ask her to tell me more. I give her solutions, when maybe she really needs a shoulder to lean on.

"I know we weren't supposed to get to the O step tonight, but while I was sharing with Josh, I just knew what I had to do. I need to go home and see if my wife will talk to me tonight. Maybe I can ask her how she feels and tell her that I want our relationship to be different. Is this a dumb idea? Am I moving too fast?"

"I'll pray for you and your wife, Michael," said Katy,

"especially in the next couple of hours. I sense it's a crucial time for you two."

"Hey," said Josh, "go for it! I'm proud of you. I know you can listen to her—like you listened to me tonight—and share with her too."

Mariana added, "I can't wait for our next class, Michael. Will you let us know how it goes?"

Michael agreed. They all shook hands as they stood, encouraging each other with smiles and nods as Mary Elizabeth announced the end of their second evening together.

CHAPTER 4

———⊳⊛⊲———

TOOLS FOR THE L STEP

*Know this, my beloved brethren. Let every man
be quick to hear, slow to speak, slow to anger.*

JAMES 1:19

WHAT ABOUT ME?

Now it's your turn to try some of the exercises that the class practiced in order to learn the first step of The L.O.V.E. Approach.

Remember, you are listening in order to understand the story that a person is telling himself or herself about a problem or issue. The person is risking much to open up to you. This kind of listening is really giving that person a gift of love.

Listening is the most crucial step in The L.O.V.E. Approach. If you listen well, you will be developing trust, which is key to building a relationship, to exploring the O, V, and E steps, and to solving the problem or issue together.

Listening is the most difficult step of the L.O.V. E. Approach. So there are as many practice exercises for the L step as you will find for all of the other three steps of The L.O.V.E. Approach combined!

Am I convinced about the importance of the L step? What are my thoughts and feelings about the verse from James at the beginning of this chapter?

PRACTICE

The **Listening and Learning Wheels** below show how Listening and Learning is similar to "turning an issue around" with cogs on a set of wheels. Listening and Learning is exploring the issue (one wheel) in relationship to a person's areas of self-awareness (a second wheel) and his or her resources (a third wheel) and needs (a fourth wheel).

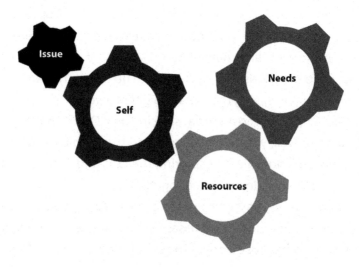

As you do this, things will look different from different angles—both to the person and to you, the listener. Listening as you "turn the issue around" helps you create a clearer picture of the person, his or her story, and how you can (eventually) proceed to the other three steps of The L.O.V.E. Approach.

This process will help the person explore the issue or problem from all angles of his own self-awareness so he will have a much fuller understanding of how the issue is affecting him. It also will help reveal to both of you that person's needs plus the resources available to tackle the issue.

Then, both you and the person you are listening to will be better able to consider the options, the new vision needed, and the practical steps to extend help and to resolve the issue or problem before you.

SELF WHEEL

The cogs of this wheel are:

1. **Feelings:** physical responses and reactions (fear, anxiety, sadness, anger, disappointment, peacefulness, happiness, etc.) that affect thoughts and actions. A feeling is neither

right nor wrong, but it can lead to actions that are right or wrong. It can be confused with thoughts ("I feel that . . ." is really a thought). Feelings are affected by thoughts, wants, values, beliefs (as well as needs and resources)—and as they are clarified, feelings may change.

2. **Thoughts:** conclusions or judgments that may be true, false, partly true, based on incorrect information, clouded by feelings, etc. ("This is my only option," "I can't handle this," "You don't care," "This is impossible," etc.); ideas ("I could do this . . .," "What if . . ."); or expectations ("I should be able to . . .," "He should . . .," "It should work this way . . .," etc.)

3. **Wants:** desires or dreams that a person holds deep in the heart ("I want to be in relationship with you," "I want to be seen as valuable," "I want to understand my purpose," "I don't want to give up," "I want to be a good parent," etc.)

4. **Values:** what a person holds most dear or worthwhile (or not) in terms of standards or qualities; what is most important to a person (faith, family, doing a good job, faithfulness, honesty, making a difference, being a good spouse/parent/friend/boss/person/Christian, etc.)

5. **Beliefs:** convictions or opinions related to religion, faith, eternal truths, or spiritual life which may or may not need clarification ("God loves me—or not," "God has a purpose for my life—or not," "Forgiveness and healing are possible—or impossible," "Prayer has power—or not," "I am worthy of respect and love—or not," etc.)

PRACTICE

Put an **F, T, W, V,** or **B** in front of each statement you might hear while Listening and Learning to designate it as a feeling, thought, want, value, or belief, or perhaps a combination.

_____ I feel that you don't care about me.

_____ I am not respected or recognized for what I do.

_____ Jesus knows my situation. No matter what I have to do, He will forgive me.

_____ No one understands what I am facing.

_____ My children will always come first, so I can never fulfill your expectations.

_____ No matter what I do or how hard I work, it's never enough to satisfy you.

_____ This is my only option.

_____ A loving God would never allow this to happen.

_____ I don't understand how we got to this point.

_____ You always have all the answers.

Note: The above ten statements illustrate the way people share their self-awareness. First, people share thoughts more readily than anything else. All of these statements are really thoughts (or judgments), and two of them are thoughts about God or Jesus (that also might be considered beliefs). There are certainly feelings, wants, values, and beliefs hiding behind the thoughts, so it is important to ask further questions to get at these other areas of self-awareness that are more difficult to share.

Second, even if a person is sharing a feeling, want, value or belief—and it is more risky to share these than to share a thought—there are most often thoughts, judgments, or additional areas of self-awareness hiding behind them, so it is important to ask further questions and allow the person to share more deeply.

PRACTICE

Take the same ten statements and write at the end of each a specific thought, feeling, want, value, or belief (or more than one) that may be behind or underneath the statement. (If you were Listening and Learning, you could ask the person sharing to "tell me more" or try to clarify what is behind or underneath the statement.) The first one is done for you as an example.

1. I feel that you don't care about me.
This is really a judgment or **thought (T)***. Behind it:* **feeling (F)** *of loneliness? Sadness? Hurt?* **Want (W)***—a more loving or more respectful relationship?* **Value (V)***—this relationship?*

2. I am not respected or recognized for what I do.

3. Jesus knows my situation. No matter what I have to do, He will forgive me.

4. No one understands what I am facing.

5. My children will always come first, so I can never fulfill your expectations.

6. No matter what I do or how hard I work, it's never enough to satisfy you.

7. This is my only option.

8. A loving God would never allow this to happen.

9. I don't understand how we got to this point.

10. You always have all the answers.

GOOD QUESTIONS TO HELP YOU DELVE DEEPER

Here are some questions you can ask to delve deeper into more areas of self-awareness as you are Listening and Learning:

- Tell me more about your situation (or about your feelings, your thoughts, your wants, your values, your beliefs).

- How did that statement/situation/event make you feel? (Did you feel angry? Did you feel sad?)

- What did you think or conclude at that point?

- What did you want deep down at that point? What do you want deep down now?

- What do you value most? Do you value the relationship? What do you hold most dear? How do you value the other person(s) involved in this situation?

- What are your religious beliefs (or beliefs about God) related to the situation/event/problem?

Note: If your question yields a "yes" or "no" answer, or a one-word or two-word answer, simply ask, "Tell me more about that" or "Help me understand more about that."

Remember, when you ask these questions, you are still listening and learning. It is not your turn to share or to go into the next steps of The L.O.V.E. Approach. The longer you can simply listen to the story of the person in front of you, the more successful you will be in building the relationship and in helping resolve the issue or problem.

Sometimes the person you are listening to will begin to explore options on his or her own, working through the issue without you having to say much at all! At other times, fully sharing and being listened to will put the person in the perfect frame of mind to listen to *you* as you lead into the O, V, and E steps.

RESOURCES AND NEEDS WHEELS

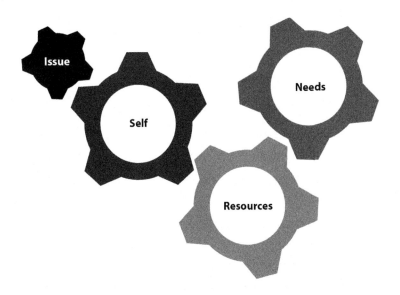

As you listen, trying to paint a fuller picture of the person and the issue before you, the person in front of you will not only reveal his or her areas of self-awareness but also his or her resources and needs.

Every person has legitimate resources and needs that are physical, emotional, intellectual, social, and spiritual.

Some of the **resources** you may hear as you listen might include recognizing that the person:

- is in a safe and healthy physical environment
- is intellectually sharp and thinking through the issue clearly
- has lots of information and tools to use in solving the problem
- has support from family and others
- is physically and emotionally strong
- is not being abused or threatened by another person
- is not addicted or mentally ill
- has a strong sense of right and wrong
- has a strong spiritual and faith foundation
- has good communication skills and can express himself or herself fully
- feels valued and loved by God and by others

Some of the needs in the person you are listening to are the reverse of these resources.

Note: At the listening stage of the process, you can make a mental note of the resources and needs you are hearing and, if appropriate, ask for clarification. For example, you could say: "Tell me more about . . . Did you say . . . Help me understand . . . Can you give me more details about . . ."

Unfortunately, especially in a crisis situation or when facing a difficult issue, many people don't recognize the resources they do have, and some people seem to have many more needs than resources.

In the O, V, and E steps, you will have additional opportunities to help the other person recognize his or her resources and needs and to provide or find the necessary help to address the issue or problem at hand.

REFLECTION
(Share your answers with your partner or small group)

What is my reaction to the Listening and Learning Wheels? Have they helped me to understand what I'm listening for when I hear another person's story?

Has the self wheel helped me to recognize different areas of self-awareness: feelings, thoughts, wants, values, beliefs?

PRACTICE
(Allow ten minutes)

Sit face-to-face with a partner who has gone through the Reflections and Practice in this chapter and is willing to share with you about an issue or problem they face and need to make a decision about.

This could be an issue such as how best to care for an elderly parent, whether to change jobs, how to deal with a problem relating to a child, whether to move or make a major purchase, whether to take a vacation right now, or how to deal with a difficult situation on the job or with a neighbor. Be sure you are willing to share somewhat intimately on this issue.

One person will be the listener and one the sharer. Before the first person starts to share, set a timer for five minutes. If you are the sharer, begin telling the listener about your issue.

If you are the listener, listen for the other person's areas of self-awareness, resources, and needs. Ask good questions to help the person share more deeply as you turn the wheels connected to the issue or problem.

If you are the listener, do NOT get into solving the problem. Don't give advice, discuss options, provide a new vision, or offer practical help and support. You must ONLY LISTEN.

When the timer goes off, change roles, and set the timer for another five minutes. Now the person who was the listener becomes the sharer. The same rules apply.

When the timer goes off, stop sharing and listening. Do not go into the O, V, and E steps with each other (you will have a chance to do that later).

REFLECTION
(Share your answers with your partner or small group)

When you were the Sharer . . .
- How did I feel being listened to?

- What did my listener say or do to help me share more fully?

- How did the experience of being listened to influence where I am in the process of dealing with my issue or solving my problem?

When you were the Listener . . .
- How did it feel to be the listener?

- Was it difficult for me to just listen and not get into the problem-solving steps (O,V,E)?

- If so, what helped me to get back on track with listening, or what tools or tips from this chapter helped me most?

- Did this exercise help me develop a relationship with the other person?

CHAPTER 5

—————✦————

MICHAEL TRIES THE L STEP

When Michael arrived home, he found his wife, Christy, sitting on the floor in their family room, papers strewn around, and working on her tablet. She didn't acknowledge his entry.

Michael started getting cold feet. He judged again that their relationship had gone too far in the wrong direction for any action of his tonight to make much of a difference. Why put his feelings out there? What if they got rejected? He'd end up feeling even worse. Maybe he should just tough it out, face the inevitable—their marriage was a mistake.

Christy's failure to even make eye contact took away the feeling of tenderness for her that had welled up in him on the drive home. She was always working, or else she was catching up with friends on social media. Suddenly he didn't feel loving at all.

But then he remembered what Mary Elizabeth had emphasized—that when you don't feel loving, you can still make a decision to love. Acting on that decision with loving words or gestures can cause loving feelings to return.

Michael remembered what had given him hope in the first

place: his own feeling of disappointment in himself during class; Dr. Meyer's sharing about his wife; the encouragement from his team, especially Josh; and Katy's promise to pray for him.

He regained some courage and tried to open a conversation. He consciously made sure he was asking his first question with a loving tone.

"Hey, Christy, do you have time to talk right now? We could just sit down here on the couch. You look busy, but maybe we could talk a little, and then you could get back to what you're doing."

For what seemed like a long time to Michael, Christy didn't raise her head, and when she did, there was a doubtful look in her eyes, but at least she made eye contact with him. She got up, walked over to the couch, and sat down. It popped into Michael's mind that maybe she was making a decision to love too. Michael sat down beside her.

Christy was looking away at something in the room, but Michael consciously keep his eyes on her face.

"We had an interesting training tonight," he started, then paused as he searched for the right way to begin. "It was all about listening and building relationships. You know, I had to do this training to be on the board of the Food Pantry, and my boss insisted . . ." Michael realized he was getting offtrack.

"Anyway, it made me think that maybe I learned something that could make our relationship better. I know we don't have much of a relationship right now. You've told me that I never listen to you, and I don't get your feelings. Now I see that. Up to now, I didn't get my own feelings. I never paid much attention to them. I always thought they were unimportant, compared to what is in my head. Anyway, I didn't understand what it means to be listened to and to share your feelings."

Michael felt his heart pounding, and he didn't know if he could go on. This was hard. But he kept looking at Christy's face. He saw her look soften as she turned her eyes toward him. He had a hard time looking her in the eye, but he did.

"I'm an accountant, a numbers guy; I'm all 'left brain' . . ." As his voice trailed off, he realized he was making excuses again.

"Let me start again. I want to tell you how I feel and what I want. I'm disappointed in myself as a husband. This is not what I want for our marriage. I feel lonely. I know I'm to blame because I really didn't understand, until tonight, that I have been shutting you out, not giving you a chance to get close or share how you feel—not just how you feel about me, but about everything that happens—on your job, with your friends, even with the news and stories you're always reading on your tablet or your phone."

A quick look that passed across Christy's face made Michael stop. He realized he was no longer talking about himself, like he wanted to; now he was blaming Christy.

"I know you've tried to share with me sometimes, and I never have time. Or I cut you off. I'm the solutions guy. But I want to do better. Will you give me a chance?"

Christy reached out and took Michael's hand.

"I can hardly believe you are saying this," said Christy, slowly and with a tentative tone. "I was feeling so angry with you when you came in tonight—you were gone; you had left me alone again." She paused for several seconds.

Michael felt a quick churning feeling in his stomach. Christy seemed to be blaming him for attending a training required for him to join the Food Pantry board, a good cause his boss supported. Didn't she realize that this would help his job?

He almost jumped in to defend himself, but he remembered that was one of his big barriers. Christy had his hand, and he saw in her eyes that she was struggling.

He read her body language. It contradicted her accusing words. *Maybe this is not about Christy blaming me,* he thought. He realized suddenly that this was his chance to learn more about her feelings. All he could think to say were those "three magic words."

"Tell me more . . . about your feelings," Michael responded, looking into her eyes.

Christy began slowly, but then the words flowed quickly. She told Michael she felt lonely when he put so many hours into work in the evenings and on weekends. She kept busy, too, but it wasn't helping. He had always seemed to have time for her before they got married. She felt distant from him. She felt closer to her friends at work than to him.

Michael became interested in what Christy was sharing. He found himself encouraging her to continue, through nodding, eye contact, and an occasional "uh-huh."

Sometimes she wondered if they would be happier together had they not married in the first place, she confessed. But, of course, she believed in marriage—both sets of parents had long marriages and were committed to each other for life. Relationships were hard; they demanded work, and she knew anything valuable demanded effort. She knew God's grace could help. She wondered if they had called on that enough in their marriage. They went to church together on Sunday, but that was about it. Maybe they needed better role models.

Maybe they could learn from other couples. Maybe there was a young couples' group at the church—or maybe the pastor could give them some advice or recommend a counselor.

Christy's words flowed smoothly while Michael just listened. He was somewhat taken aback by everything Christy shared. Being analytical, he realized that she was sharing not only her feelings, but also her thoughts, values, and beliefs. She shared some of her needs and resources. She was also offering solutions to their problems. And many of these he agreed with.

Then she stopped and looked at him intently, as if waiting for him to respond.

Michael suddenly remembered something else he learned in class. Wants are often the most difficult thing for people to share. They are very intimate and often closely held. Would Christy risk sharing her wants with him?

He asked her softly, "What do you really want in our relationship?"

At that, Christy teared up and she squeezed Michael's hand even harder. "I know I don't want it to end. I really want us to recapture what we felt for each other when we decided to get married. We wanted to spend time together, share our lives.

"I want us to put each other first, not last. I want us to be more unselfish—how else can we commit for all the ups and downs of life, in the future, as we get older, as we have kids. I want us to be strong together so we can be good parents . . ."

Michael put his arms around her, and they were quiet for a while. Michael didn't want to spoil the moment.

He finally made eye contact again and said sincerely, "I want the same things. I love you. You laid out a lot of options for us to get some help. I'm usually the problem solver, but you had most of ideas this time!" he said with a smile. "Let's not talk anymore about our options tonight. There'll be time for us to make a plan so we don't get into this rut again. I never want to feel hopeless again about us."

"Well, we can't discuss this tomorrow night. It will have to be another time," Christy responded. Raising her eyebrows and opening her eyes wide, she said, "I don't want you to miss that class!"

"We'll figure it out . . . together," concluded Michael, taking both of her hands. "Do you want to get back to what you were doing when I came in?" he asked tentatively.

"It's not that important now," Christy said, smiling.

CHAPTER 6

———————

CLASS THREE—THE O STEP
OPEN OPTIONS

The students began gathering into their groups of four for the third class, engaging in some animated conversations as they took their chairs and opened their notebooks. A slide was already projected on the screen:

> **L** = Listen and Learn
> **O** = **Open Options**
> **V** = Vision and Value
> **E** = Extend and Empower

"You all know the focus of tonight's class," began Mary Elizabeth. "But before we begin with the O step of The L.O.V.E. Approach, I'm wondering if some of you tried the L step last night. Would anyone be willing to share with the bigger group, especially if something you learned in our last class was really helpful?"

Several people shared, and many of their experiences were with family members. Michael raised his hand too. His teammates, knowing that he had gone home the night before with a heavy—but hopeful—heart, listened intently.

"I had a conversation with my wife last night that was really different—thanks to what I learned in the class, plus encouragement from my group," Michael said, as he nodded to Josh, Mariana, and especially Katy who had promised to pray for him.

"It was awkward at first. I had to intentionally stop myself so I didn't interrupt or plan what to say next." Michael smiled as he heard some sympathetic chuckles.

"I made a decision to love, be quiet, and use the 'three magic words.' Noticing our body language really helped too. We did start to do some problem solving—at least throwing out some options to our problem that all sounded good. So maybe I don't need the class tonight? But my wife says I can't miss any of the training. She already likes the results!"

As Michael sat down, Mariana and Katy smiled and nodded. Josh gave him a grin and friendly slap on the back.

"It's not always possible to come up with good options to resolve a problem as quickly and naturally as Michael and his wife were able to last night," said Mary Elizabeth, with a smile. "So tonight we're going to explore the Options process in more detail, step by step.

"Would you agree with this? People often make decisions they regret. Let's look at why," Mary Elizabeth suggested, as she switched to the next slide. Seven factors slowly rolled onto the screen.

7 Reasons People Choose an Option They Later Regret
- Intense feelings (so they can't process the options clearly).
- Fear and uncertainty (so they don't act at all).
- Either/Or thinking (so they can't see both/and, or multiple options).
- Poor understanding of the pros and cons of each option.

- Options don't match their own values and beliefs.
- Pressure/coercion (so they cannot choose freely).
- Perceived lack of support (so they rule out certain options).

"As confirmed by research, along with common sense, these obstacles can block a person's ability to choose the best option when faced with challenging issues and problems. The good news is that someone like YOU can help a person overcome these obstacles. See the next slide."

4 Factors That Characterize a Better Option:
- It is well **thought-out**.
- It is consistent with their true **values and beliefs**.
- They **feel** free to choose it (no anger, fear, pressure, coercion).
- They have the **resources** and support they **need** (it is doable).

"It's the Listening and Learning Wheels again!" whispered Michael to Josh.

It was an aha moment for many others in the room as well.

"Do those words in bold look familiar? **Thoughts, feelings, values, beliefs, needs,** and **resources** are what you are listening for and learning about in the L step of The L.O.V.E. Approach.

"As you work on the O step with another person, you continue to listen. And you use what you learn to help the person see how their own areas of self-awareness plus their resources and needs match up with the potential options.

"To truly help another person choose an option he or she feels good about—or, if the two of you are involved in the problem, an option that you *both* feel good about—we need first to examine our habits as problem solvers."

5 Problem-Solving Behaviors

- The Coach/Partner—I'll be involved with you step-by-step.
- The Bystander—I'll observe, but it's totally up to you.
- The Analyzer—I'll tell you all the pros and cons.
- The Right Answer Man—I'll tell you exactly what to do.
- The Buddy or BFF—I'll support you whatever you decide.

"Can anyone guess, just by these short descriptions, which is the most effective problem-solving behavior if we are trying to help a person find the option that meets the criteria we have discussed tonight?" asked Mary Elizabeth.

There were some murmurs in the room, along with glances and quick exchanges between partners and among the groups.

"Sometimes we might think we need someone who just tells us what to do or supports us no matter what, but it's really a person who takes the Coach/Partner role who will be most helpful in the O step of the The L.O.V.E. Approach because that role includes a high level of personal involvement."

Mariana raised her hand. "Just wondering—aren't there cases where there is only one right way? I mean, what if someone thinks something is an option, but it's totally wrong? Maybe it would really hurt them or someone else; maybe it's even life or death. You mean I shouldn't be the Right Answer Man even then?" asked Mariana, revealing the behavior she immediately identified with.

"That's a complex question," answered Mary Elizabeth. "Telling a person what is best to do or not to do is not as effective as helping that person come to see what is best, with your loving help, through careful processing of the options. You can help him come to his own conclusion that a particular option is not good for him, or perhaps for other people in his life. Or that it is not God's plan for him. God's plan is always to prosper us, not to harm us—to give us hope and a future.

"Envision—or help someone see or discover—not tell, is the best way to share the truth in love. You can begin doing that in the O step simply by being objective and accurate about the pros and cons of each option.

"We will discuss this even more fully in the V step when it is your turn to share a new Vision and Value with the other person. That's often the best time to share the truth in love. So hold that thought for our class tomorrow night."

Mary Elizabeth instructed the class to turn to the "What About Me" section of their workbook, reflect on their own problem-solving behaviors, and then gather in their small groups and share their responses.

The entire class worked diligently. The length of time they needed to complete the exercise indicated that they could identify with multiple roles.

When it was time to get together in their group of four, Mariana jumped in first.

"I'm a Right Answer Man, as you heard," said Mariana. "Most of the time I know right away what the alternatives are and which one we—or even the other person—should take. I don't hesitate to say so. I don't change my behaviors very much, no matter who it is with the problem. At least I'm consistent. But I'm not proud of the way I act, and it isn't working with my employees. I'd like to be a Coach—maybe I can learn."

Josh chuckled when he began to share, but the group could

tell it was to cover up some discomfort. "Like I said before, sometimes I'm so distracted with multitasking that I'm like the Bystander. I kind of watch from the sideline even when someone shares a problem with me—and sometimes I try to lighten things up to get a laugh so I can move on."

"I'm kind of the BFF," said Katy. "I just bond with other people; my heart goes out to them. I'm as confused as they are, and I don't know how to sort things out with them. I hope I can learn!"

Michael looked thoughtful. "I'm almost always the Analyzer—really good at checking off every possible alternative with the pros and cons. But last night, when my wife was throwing out options for us, I didn't rush into analyzing them—I wanted to just focus on her, on us. On the people, not just the problem. That's a change, and it felt good. When the time is right, I want to discuss the options to improve our relationship. I hope that's a step toward being a Partner."

Calling the group back to order, Mary Elizabeth moved to the next important lesson, which she put up on the screen.

Be Relational as You Open Options

"As you learned in reflecting on your problem-solving behaviors, only one of the roles we looked at is truly relational, and that's the Coach/Partner. Interaction, being involved, and doing so in a loving, caring, patient way (remember 1 Corinthians) is crucial when you help someone process options.

"It's service, love in action, because it involves making yourself (your time, energy, talents) a gift to the other person.

"Any other role you take will leave the problem solving

almost totally up to the other person. That's lonely, and it may result in a decision that the other person (or even both of you) will later regret.

"Here are five concrete ways of being relational when you discuss options with another person," said Mary Elizabeth, moving to the next slide and giving instructions for the class to turn to the appropriate section of their notebooks.

5 Relationship-Building Tips for the O Step
1. Be factual, informative, and objective (non-emotional).
2. Be involved and active.
3. Be person-centered.
4. Be personal.
5. Be loving, caring, and nonjudgmental.

"Please study the descriptions of these behaviors carefully in your notebooks, then complete the exercises that give you practice in discussing sensitive matters in a relational way. I'll let you know when it's time to share what you have done with your partner.

"If you don't learn to open options in this relational way, you will sound like that 'noisy gong' or 'clanging cymbal'—like the Right Answer Man or the Analyzer. Or you won't be much help at all—like the Bystander or the Buddy or BFF. And don't forget what your body language may be saying, even silently!"

The students worked diligently through several exercises, sharing willingly when it came time to work with their partners. It was time for the break.

When the break was over, the group saw that Dr. Meyer had joined them.

"Welcome back, Dr. Meyer. I'd like the class to hear the next part of your story. I've been stressing how the O step must be interactive and relational. Your coach really did a great job with both!"

"Thanks, Mary Elizabeth, and good to be with you all again. Last night I told you about meeting with my old coach and our coffee together. I don't really believe in coincidences, only God-incidences, and this sure was one! In that brief time, Coach really listened to me and was able to discern and reflect back to me not only some of my major needs, but also some of my resources, and he did it by drawing out my story, through my feelings, thoughts, wants, values, and beliefs. Using the Listening and Learning Wheels had become second nature to him.

"When we were both ready to engage in discussing my options, we met again, this time at his office. He began by asking me if I had thought much about the options I had. I told him that my anxiety was back and that I still felt like I was in a rut. I told him that my choices still seemed equally bad—an either/or. I could stay in a job I felt more and more unsuited for that was making me miserable—or I could quit and throw my family into financial chaos.

"Coach listened quietly, encouraging me to finish what I had to say, and then he asked me if I had ever heard of an Options Tree. I had not."

Dr. Meyer turned to the whiteboard, picked up a marker, and started to draw. "Coach used the whiteboard in his office, and he drew an Options Tree with the two options I said I had."

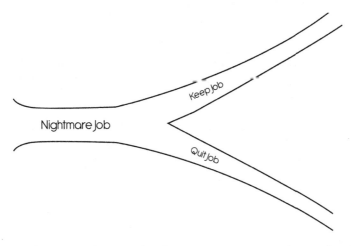

"Then Coach started asking me questions about the first branch: keep my job. He asked me what I thought would happen down the road if I continued on that path. We put lots of branches on that limb—I could think mainly of cons, and so could he," said Dr. Meyer, continuing to draw on the whiteboard.

"Coach pointed out how this alternative clearly conflicted

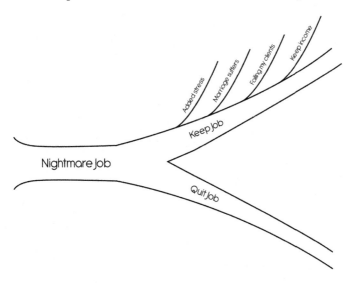

with some of my core values—especially the value I placed on my marriage and the standards of my profession. The other branch—quit my job—had cons too," Dr. Meyer said, adding more lines to the Options Tree on the whiteboard. "What would happen? Again, some of the consequences, like going into major debt and putting such strain on my wife and children, went against my core values."

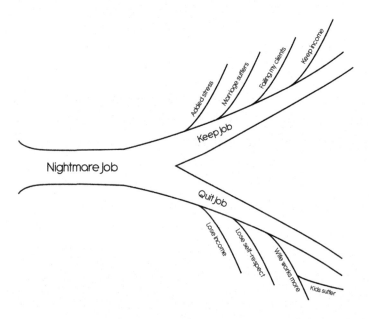

"Coach then asked if there could be another option we had not yet thought of. We put our heads together, almost literally. He was patient, reminding me of several things I had told him over our coffee together, some of my feelings and wants, some of my resources and needs. We started drawing a third limb—this one had cons too, but also some pros." Dr. Meyer continued drawing on the board.

"Some things on the diagram needed more research—exact

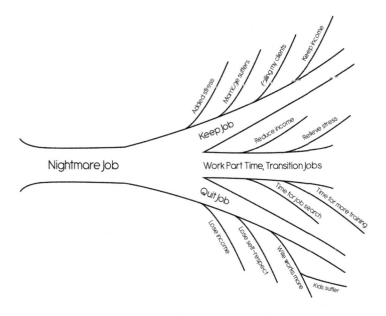

financial figures, for instance. But here was a third option, working part time while I transitioned to a different job or career, that I had not considered before—and it had possibilities! I was encouraged!

"I copied the Options Tree in a notebook that I took home and shared with my wife. I could see that she needed to be a full partner in helping map out the options and fill in the details.

"It took several additional meetings, with my wife joining Coach and me, before we came up with a real plan. But I'll tell you more about that tomorrow evening, when you move into the next step of The L.O.V.E. Approach."

The trainees gave Dr. Meyer a hand as he stepped down, and Mary Elizabeth took the podium again.

"All of you analytical types in the class are looking excited about getting to draw Options Trees, but I can see that the rest of you are looking a little glassy-eyed right now. This kind of diagramming is just one way of trying to sort through the pros and cons of options and process how they relate to a person's feelings, thoughts, wants, values, beliefs, needs, and resources.

"You can process in a similar way with circles, bubbles, doodles, lists, outlines, or notes. Occasionally it all becomes clear merely through good discussion—without writing anything down!"

Mary Elizabeth instructed the class to remember the issue or problem they had shared with their partner the evening before and remember their experience of truly being listened to by their partner. They had not been allowed to move into problem solving—only listen.

"It's time now to get back to the issues you identified in the L step and help each other open options. Open your notebooks, and let's get busy!"

Mariana and Katy quickly started working together, sorting through options—Mariana for how to handle the issue with her problem employee and Katy with her leadership of the women's ministry small group. Josh and Michael focused on sorting through Josh's options involving his son and Michael's options with his wife.

When it was time for the four of them to share, they all had a good laugh when Michael and Josh held up neat and logical Options Trees, thanks to Michael's leadership. Mariana showed her detailed outline with Roman numerals and As, Bs, Cs. Then Katy revealed her drawing, featuring interconnected circles— which the team voted "most original"!

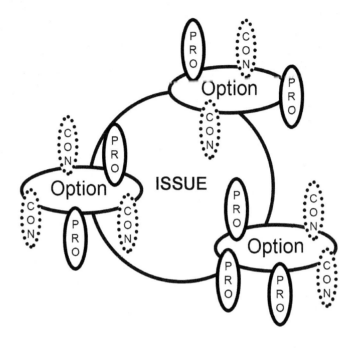

All four felt encouraged. They understood more fully their choices, and they all saw a potential way forward on the issues they were facing.

But Mariana was the most excited. "I want to work more on this tonight after I get home. I'm going to meet as soon as possible tomorrow with my employee. I owe him more of my time. I want to be more of a Coach than a dictator," she said, smiling, "and I think this is my chance to try."

Our four decided to end the evening with their heads bowed, asking for God's help, especially for Mariana while she tried the O step.

CHAPTER 7

———∞———

TOOLS FOR THE O STEP

For I know the plans I have for you, says the Lord, plans for
welfare and not for evil, to give you a future and a hope.
JEREMIAH 29:11

WHAT ABOUT ME?

Helping another person delve into the various options available
to resolve an issue or problem (especially if the problem involves
you in some way!) requires that you become engaged in a
process that can be demanding and time-consuming. Opening
options is an active process!

Think about a time recently when someone shared a problem
with you—perhaps someone in the family or at church has
mentioned a financial issue or an issue with a child, friend, or
fellow employee. Perhaps the person even said something like
"What would you do in that case?" What was your "go to" behavior?

Or perhaps you were the person who shared such an issue with
a friend or family member. What was that person's "go to" behavior?

Most of these behaviors allow us to "move on" and avoid

engagement with the other person. Put a checkmark in front of the behaviors below that you personally have used when someone shares a problem or issue with you. If there is a specific person that you often use this behavior with, or situation where you commonly use this behavior, indicate that in the space underneath the behavior.

5 Problem-Solving Behaviors

1. _____ The Coach/Partner (who comes alongside and offers helpful feedback as you move along step-by-step).

2._____ The Bystander (who observes the situation somewhat from a distance).

3._____ The Analyzer (who tells you all the pros and cons of your options).

4._____ The Right Answer Man (who knows the "right" way to proceed and will immediately tell you what to do and why you should do it).

5._____ The Buddy or BFF (who immediately gives you his or her support for "whatever you decide").

What am I learning about my own behaviors when someone shares an issue or problem with me?

Is there something I need to work on in my own behavior in order to truly help someone else in opening options?

NOTE: EXPERTISE IN OPENING OPTIONS

You may have the role of opening options as an "expert" in a particular field. For example, the four characters in our story, Michael, Mariana, Josh, and Katy, have different roles in the organizations where they volunteer or work. If Josh is expected to use the O step with a fatherless boy at the King Ranch who has a drug problem, he will need to become an "expert" in options that people with drug addictions need to know about. He will need to learn a great deal of information on the physical, mental, and spiritual effects of drug use on the individual and family, details about the variety of treatment options, support options, opportunities for financial help, residential care, out-patient programs, and so on.

If you are not an expert in the options that could be discussed, you can still help the person create an Options Tree and discuss options in a general way. Later, in the E step, you can find experts and expert information to assist in the process.

Whether you are an expert or not, you should discuss the options in what we call a "relational" way.

5 RELATIONSHIP-BUILDING TIPS

1. **Be factual, informative, and objective (non-emotional).** Don't be afraid to say that you don't know or aren't sure

about certain information related to an option. Offer to help find out more if you continue in the coach/partner relationship. Share as much as you honestly can, given your own expertise and experience. Emotional, rather than factual, language may frighten the other person. Emotional language can cause him or her to block out crucial information, question the value of the information, or begin to distrust you.

2. **Be involved and active.** If you have or know of videos, brochures, pamphlets, websites that contain valuable information related to an option, present this information person to person. Go over these kinds of resources WITH the other person if at all possible, paying attention to how the information is being received. Notice the feelings, thoughts, wants, values, and beliefs of the other person, as in the Listening and Learning Wheels.

3. **Be person-centered.** Make sure the person knows you are focusing on him or her, not just on information related to the options. For example, continue to pay attention to body language, maintain good eye contact, and keep listening and learning for new insights as you discuss options. Be responsive to what you learned about the other person in the L step. If there is something about one of the options that relates to the Listening and Learning Wheels, connect what you learned about the person to one or more of the options.

4. **Be personal.** If you have experiences or stories related to the situation or issue, or to one of the options, you may want to share them. But remember, this is not about YOU or any other person than the one sitting in front of or

beside you. If your story would distract the other person or turn attention to yourself rather than give insight to an option, this is not the time to share it.

5. **Be loving, caring, and nonjudgmental.** Show that you care about the person in front of or beside you and what they are going through. Remember the behavior Paul described in 1 Corinthians 13. You may consider some of the other person's past actions or the options he or she is considering to be dangerous or even immoral. You can share more about God's plan for this person in the V step. But as you initially go over all the possible options, let your behavior show that you are making distinctions between actions or options (which can clearly be morally right or wrong) and the person (whom only God can judge).

Note: Practice these behavior tips not only in your verbal communication, but also through your nonverbals!

PRACTICE

The following are the kinds of statements that might be made when one person is discussing options and their pros and cons with another person. Which of the five relationship-building characteristics do you notice in each of the statements? For example, if a statement is factual and objective (non-emotional) and also person-centered, put both a 1 and a 3 on the line after that statement. If none of the above characteristics is present, put a 0.

1. Every time we meet about your sales results, I've mentioned that you could video your presentation and get someone on the team to point out what you're doing wrong. Have you done that yet? _____

2. Honey, I found these in your room when I was putting away your clothes. Dad and I are really concerned that you, or one of your friends, or both of you, may be involved in something that could cause you lasting harm. Before we sat down with you, we looked up a few videos online that explain in detail the dangers along this path, and we want to look at them with you. From the tears in your eyes, it looks like you know you're in over your head. We are here to help you sort out your options. _____

3. You have thought of lots of things you could do, and you can pursue more than one at a time. One of your options is Al-Anon. Someone in our family is an alcoholic, too, so I can relate to the suffering you are going through and the feeling of confusion and hopelessness you shared with me. I find so much help and support when I go to Al-Anon meetings. Maybe I can take you to the meeting I go to, and you can check it out. _____

4. Thank you for coming to me right after you saw the doctor— you know I had a similar diagnosis a few years ago. I see the concern on your face. I want to go over all the brochures and fact sheets you have in your hand. I don't know everything about all these treatment options, but I can help you go over this information and seek out more if you want to. First, though, tell me how you are feeling right now. _____

5. Yes, that is an option. But the results would be devastating—emotional trauma, broken hearts, the end of your dreams, destruction of trust, a waste of everything you've worked for. . . . It's just wrong. _____

6. Like you say, none of your choices seem good. Staying in your present position gives you the most security, but you've said you're feeling really uncomfortable with the office ethics. High ethical standards are one of the things you value most. I was in a situation like that once, but it solved itself when one of the people moved on. I have a friend who is a human resources executive. If you want, I could outline your situation and see if you have an obligation to report this, and if you do, what could happen. _____

PRACTICE

Go back to the listening exercise you did with your partner and shared in your small group in chapter 4. Use the skills you just practiced to explore possible options for the issues or problems and to create an Options Tree for each person. Work as partners and then in your small group.

Remember, it sometimes seems that there are only two options with an issue or problem: 1) doing nothing—continuing on the same path that you are on, or 2) choosing a radically different path. However, there is often a third option that takes a little more time to discern. Or, one of the two main options may actually branch into other options as you discuss what could happen next or what options might later present themselves.

If you prefer, instead of an Options Tree, you can create outlines (if your team is "left brain"-oriented). Or write down words, ideas, sketches, or even "doodles" as they come to you in brainstorming, then connect related things with circles, lines, and dots (if your team is "right brain"-oriented). Or you can create your own way of putting all the options on paper.

Try to make your diagram simple and clear, and not too complex.

MY OPTIONS TREE, OPTIONS OUTLINE, OR SKETCH

REFLECTION
(Share your answers with your partner or small group)

Did I settle on an option for my issue or problem that had the 4 Factors That Characterize a Better Option as discussed in chapter 6?

What did my partner or small group say or do that helped me in creating my Options Tree (or alternative drawing of options)? Did he or she use some of the 5 Relationship-Building Tips from this chapter? If so, which ones? How did that help me?

How did I try to help my partner or small group create their Options Trees (or alternative drawings of options)? Did I try to use some of the 5 Relationship-Building Tips from this chapter? Did I intentionally focus on my nonverbal communication too? Which tips seemed to be most helpful?

CHAPTER 8

MARIANA TRIES THE O STEP

Mariana had thought through the options she had for dealing with her problem employee Tomas the night before in her small group. From thinking she had only two—let Tomas go or hold his feet to the fire with constant directives and oversight until he meets his assigned goals—she realized she had a third. She had committed to try to coach Tomas, using what she had learned about The L.O.V.E. Approach, first listening and then working with him to see if together they could come up with ways to resolve whatever was causing him to fail.

Her outline of how she would approach the coaching had given her confidence the night before, as had the prayers of her team. This morning, after she scheduled Tomas to come to her office for another review and problem-solving session, she was not quite so sure she was prepared. She loved new challenges, but she had never used this method of problem solving in the "real world"; she had only used it in the classroom. She knew it would be awkward at first.

But she didn't want to revert to being the Right Answer Man. That hadn't gotten her very far with Tomas up to this point anyway, and if she had to spend time replacing him, the capital campaign would have to be extended and might never meet its overall goal. She would fail too.

Her thoughts were interrupted when she heard a knock on her office door. She made sure she had a smile on her face and made eye contact with Tomas as she welcomed him into her office. She motioned him toward one of the only chairs she had, on the other side of her big desk, suddenly realizing for the first time that it seemed very formal, even imposing. She wished she had thought of that before. She probably needed a less intimidating meeting space if she wanted to try this coaching thing. She hadn't thought of water or coffee either. That might have helped put Tomas at ease.

Tomas sat, his shoulders drooping and his eyes focused on a manila folder he was clutching on his lap. Mariana had never paid much attention to his body language before; she had always wanted to jump right into her agenda. She wondered if that was normal for him or if it signaled discouragement. He probably hadn't made much progress toward his goals yet. Probably he was expecting another reprimand. Mariana thought she'd better start with some encouragement.

"Thanks for coming in this morning, Tomas. I know we hadn't planned another meeting to go over your numbers until next week—they probably haven't changed much . . ." Mariana stopped, aware that this wasn't a very encouraging opening. Tomas didn't look up, so she started again.

"Tomas, I haven't been much of a help as you've struggled to meet the numerical objectives in the last month or so. But I hope that can change. I haven't given you a chance to tell me what is really happening when you try to work the plan. I've simply told you to work harder, or longer. I want to listen to you now. I want to help figure out what is going on and see what we can come up with together. I care about the bottom line, that's true. The campaign has to be successful for the future of the church. But I care about you and your success too."

Tomas looked so vulnerable, sitting there. He was the youngest member of her admin team. She was at least twice his age. She really did care about him, as a person, as a staff member . . . as a brother in Christ.

"I haven't paid enough attention to you," Mariana continued, her voice trailing off as she realized how her focus on the task alone—a big financial challenge in her new role as church administrator—had caused her to forget the young man in front of her. How could that have happened? Paul's Letter to the Corinthians came to mind—the noisy gong, the clanging cymbal.

As Mariana paused, Tomas looked up, and she saw relief on his face, although she sensed he was still a little doubtful. She refocused on the new task at hand, smiled at Tomas, and said warmly, "Please tell me what is happening as you have been trying to work the plan." Thinking of the Listening and Learning Wheels, Mariana continued, "Start anyplace you want. Tell me what you are thinking and feeling. Tell me if there are needs you see. Maybe resources you don't have but that might be available . . ."

Tomas began slowly but then quickened his pace as he described all the steps he had taken and the hours he had put in. He then started enumerating the obstacles that he encountered along the way. He shared how his feelings had gone from excitement about being able to impact the church and being trusted with leading this part of the campaign to overwhelming discouragement and frustration when nothing seemed to be working.

At times it was difficult for Mariana to keep herself from jumping in to offer a potential solution to one or more of the obstacles, but she forced herself to stick to open-ended statements such as "Tell me more about that." She thought that what Tomas needed most now was encouragement, and she sensed he was getting that from her good eye contact and nods. She wanted to be a good listener and build their relationship, and then perhaps they could tackle this problem together.

She became more and more impressed with Tomas' tenacity as he described the steps he had taken, and she came to the surprising conclusion that he had been unsuccessful in achieving his goals not because he hadn't worked hard or long enough but because the fundraising plan itself was not right for their church.

"Tomas," she said, after she had given him a chance to totally download all that had been happening, "I want to apologize. I can't think of anything that can be improved in your execution of the plan. The steps you followed are supposed to be the best practices—recruit volunteers, deliver the campaign packets, ask for the gifts person-to-person, and then follow up. From what I've heard you say, it's just not working. But the cause is not poor implementation. It may be the plan itself."

Mariana got up from her desk and moved toward the whiteboard, and Tomas turned his chair in that direction. "Let's look at the only two options I gave you—until today," she said, drawing what looked like a tree. At first it had only two major branches. On the first branch she wrote *Work current plan harder* and on the second, *Get someone else to work the plan.*

She looked at Tomas, and they smiled at each other. Tomas leaned toward the board with an intense look on his face. Obviously, they needed better options, and they were both intent on finding them.

MarIana consciously made the decision not to move too quickly. She wanted to transition from her go-to problem-solving behavior, the Right Answer Man, to being the Coach and processing the options with Tomas.

She started drawing lines out from the first branch, and she asked Tomas to help her think of the pros and cons of the current plan. There was one big pro: there was value in one-to-one personal contact, in volunteers connecting with other church members. But the cons were numerous, and Tomas easily ticked them off: volunteers not able to devote the time; driving distances (church members came from fifty-six zip codes); people weren't home for deliveries; people don't answer their phones; a younger church demographic; and more.

Mariana started drawing other branches on the tree, confident that she and Tomas would be able to label them with options that had not been tried. Surely there were alternate ways of getting the word out to the members and receiving their support. Coming from the corporate world, this was Mariana's first experience with a nonprofit capital campaign, but she did know a lot about communications and sales. She was sure those had something to do with fundraising.

Tomas pulled out his cell phone and announced that if it was OK with Mariana, he would start searching for church capital campaigns. He quickly pulled up several articles, glanced at titles, and asked Mariana if he could come up to the whiteboard and add some labels. When she eagerly agreed, he labeled one branch *crowd sourcing,* another *pastor open houses,* and a third *social media and Facebook.*

As they continued to work together, it was clear that these alternate options had their own pros and cons, but neither Mariana nor Tomas could confidently diagram them. The decision of how to proceed was still unclear. They were at a standstill. That was a little frustrating to Mariana since she prided herself at being able to quickly find the right answer. This whole situation with Tomas was humbling.

Mariana said, "Let's sit down again and think about this." They both sat, looking at the Options Tree they had created. It had several branches with "twigs," but there were details they still needed in order to really make a new plan.

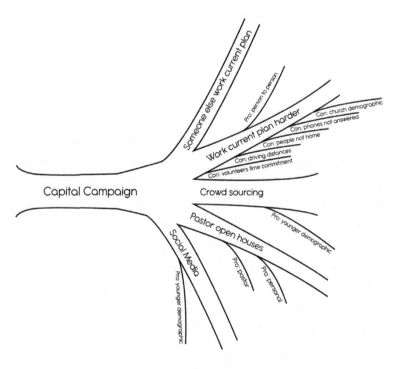

Mariana remembered that Mary Elizabeth had warned the class that some options discussions need the input of an expert, not just brainstorming and research on the internet.

"I think we have done the best job we can do at this point," she told Tomas. "Our next step, in order to develop a real plan, is to contact a church fundraising expert, or maybe more than one, to help us sort out our options given what we now know about our own church community, what has not worked, and why. What do you think, Tomas?"

"Agreed," Tomas said with a nod and a smile. "Some of the companies listed in the internet articles might have consultants here, or they might even work remotely, and I could call three or four churches in the community that have done renovations in the last few years and see if they used consultants, get some recommendations, even costs. I could give you a report by Friday."

Mariana was impressed by Tomas' attitude, and she had a new appreciation for his work ethic and ability to lay out next steps. She stood up and put out her hand to shake his, wanting to give him some additional encouragement. "Good plan, Tomas. I appreciate your can-do attitude. Email me your report on Friday morning. I'll look it over, and we can proceed from there."

As Tomas left the office, he turned back, looked Mariana in the eye, and said, "I know how important this campaign is to the future of our church. I'm passionate about the vision our pastor has shared."

Tomas started almost shyly, but then he seemed to gain confidence, and Mariana noticed that he was standing straight and tall. "I want to do my job well and help our team be a success. Thank you for letting me learn from you."

Mariana knew they both had lots of work ahead, but she felt good about their progress today, about Tomas' potential—and about her own potential as a Coach/Partner for the people God had placed under her authority.

CHAPTER 9

⸺⟫●⟪⸺

CLASS FOUR—THE V STEP
VISION AND VALUE

When our four were seated together, Mariana quickly brought them up to speed. Yes, she and her problem employee had met since their last class.

"I think it worked! We even did an Options Tree together! And I wasn't the one who laid out all the options. It's great not to be facing a stalemate or looking for a replacement."

Mariana paused and took a breath. "Best of all, I feel better about myself—I am becoming a Coach, I hope, not an Answer Man. Thanks for your prayers and encouragement."

Michael, Katy, and Josh were happy for her. Katy wondered aloud if she would also have the courage to try The L.O.V.E. Approach if the opportunity presented itself. She hoped for an opportunity soon, before she lost her good intentions. Josh wanted to try it too—but he doubted if his son would open up, no matter what.

Mary Elizabeth called the group together, welcomed them back, and directed their attention to the screen:

L = Listen and Learn
O = Open Options
V = Vision and Value
E = Extend and Empower

"It sounds like some of you have already tried the O step outside the classroom—using the L step first, of course," she said with a smile. "Sometimes it is relatively easy for a person, especially with a good helper like you, to lay out all their options, the way we practiced last night. The best option becomes perfectly clear, and you can confirm their choice. You're confident that the option meets the criteria we learned earlier," said Mary Elizabeth, returning to a previous slide.

4 Factors That Characterize a Better Option
- It is well **thought-out**.
- It is consistent with their **values and beliefs**.
- They **feel** free to choose it (no anger, fear, pressure, coercion).
- They have the **resources** and support they **need** (it is doable).

"If you are personally involved in the problem—if it is a problem within the family or on a work team—the option chosen must, of course, be agreeable to you too.

"If it meets all these criteria, then the vision you share in the next step of The L.O.V.E. Approach may be really simple, something like 'You can do it, and I'm here to help' or 'Together, I know we can do this!'"

Mary Elizabeth switched to the next slide:

Encouragement!
Affirmation!

"We call that kind of vision-sharing simply 'encouragement' or 'affirmation'! Everybody needs this, especially when trying something new or making a decision to move ahead on something they've struggled with. And, they'll probably continue to need it, so keep up those encouraging words!

"Look for something specific you can affirm—the other person's gifts, skills, personality, accomplishments, or more—and then do it! Even if you think the trait is obvious, people facing problems are generally thinking more about what they lack—and less about the gifts they have.

"Simple affirmations are statements like 'You have the brains to figure this out' or 'You're a hard worker' or 'I've seen how generous you are' or 'your smile lights up a room,' 'you have always been a good example,' and so much more! These simple statements affirm the value of the person.

"The V step gets more difficult when the person you're problem solving with is seriously considering options you know are harmful—to that person's physical, mental, or even spiritual health. That person may be rejecting some better choices. Sometimes, fear, pressure, shame, or other complex factors make dangerous options more attractive.

"In the O step, you can bring up the dangers of certain options in an objective and factual way, as we learned last evening. In the V step, you can do even more to keep positive options 'on the table.'

"We are all Christians in this room, so we all agree that there is one truth, and God created human beings to seek and know that truth. Jesus is the way, the truth, and the life. God's plan—God's truth carried out in God's way—is ultimately the best way. It results in what is good for us—in this life and in the next. Let's look at the V step now," Mary Elizabeth said, bringing the group's attention to the next slide.

Share the Truth in Love

"This must be done very carefully, wisely, with the guidance of the Holy Spirit! In the V step, it can again be a temptation to be the Right Answer Man—perhaps by immediately quoting Bible verses, Christian authors, or even reading from a question-and-answer book such as a catechism. But doing this will likely break the relationship if done in the wrong way or done too soon in the relationship-building process. Then you will have little influence on the other person's choice.

"Instead of just 'being right,' let The L.O.V.E. Approach, especially the V step, help you gently guide someone you care about into making right choices—for this life and for eternal life too!"

All eyes were on Mary Elizabeth as she shared. The group was tuned into her every word. They had mostly avoided really thorny issues when they had chosen what to share with one another in class, so most of them weren't facing such difficult and sensitive discussions in their small groups.

But they could relate to what Mary Elizabeth was saying. They knew many families in their churches or organizations—even some of their own families—who were facing especially challenging issues. Some of those present were in relationship with people involved in drugs, pornography, and other addictions, or victims of abuse, neglect, or gender confusion.

As thoughts were trailing in these directions, Mary Elizabeth brought them back to the moment. "Here is a gentle, loving message—vision and value—most people need to hear, but especially when they are wounded and in morally difficult situations," said Mary Elizabeth, as she clicked on the next slide.

Vision of Self: Who Am I?
You are created in the image and likeness of God.
You are worthy of love and respect.
You are a unique creation, made for a purpose.

"Many people you will use The L.O.V.E. Approach with, in your church, at work, in your circle of friends, and in your own family, are feeling worthless and insignificant. They have been bruised and broken. In that condition, they may be allowing themselves to be used, treated as objects rather than as persons with innate dignity and value. They may have made bad, even sinful choices. They are believing all the negative names and messages that others have given them. So, you have a tremendous opportunity to share this life-giving vision of self.

"Plus, you may also have the opportunity to introduce a hurting person to a new vision of God as well. He is our loving Father—who is always pursuing us, who welcomes us when we turn to Him, as the father does in the familiar Parable of the Prodigal Son."

Mary Elizabeth touched the clicker. After the "Vision of Self" slide, the following words "Vison of God" scrolled onto the screen. The two messages of hope were side by side.

Vision of God: Who Is God?
God is a God of mercy, forgiveness, healing, and redemption.
God helps YOU when you call on Him.
God's grace is sufficient.

Mary Elizabeth studied the class to make sure that everyone was following her. All eyes were on the slides with the two powerful messages. Several people were gently nodding their heads.

"While it is difficult for some people to believe that these messages apply to them, your loving manner, your faith in them, your patience, and perhaps your personal stories will help.

"When I am using The L.O.V.E. Approach, I almost always ask the other person if I can pray for them, or if we can pray together about the issue or problem—right then and there! I have never had a person say 'no' to that offer!

"Sometimes, there is another message, a new vision or value, that you may be led to share. That vision is the answer to the questions below, and the answers are specific to the problem, issue, or even to a particular option being considered.

Is There a Better Way? God's Plan
What Would Jesus Do (WWJD) in this situation?
What is God's plan in this situation?

"Here's a specific example. Many of us have elderly parents, neighbors, or friends. Some of them may be in assisted living arrangements, nursing homes, or hospice care. If someone is facing decisions about end-of-life care, even wondering about the 'world's plan' of assisted suicide or mercy killing, you may be able to give them some actual guidance on God's plan in the V step.

"This is best done, of course, in a loving, not didactic or 'preachy,' way—perhaps with a personal story. When my family cared for our mother in her final months, we were able, with much prayer and support, to relieve her suffering by ministering to her physical, emotional, and spiritual needs. We found that personal ministry to the suffering and dying was not only possible, but it bore rich fruit—peace for our mother, deeper love within our family, and wonder at God's mercies. I have shared the details of that story with many people, and it has given them hope.

"However, many issues, even some cases in care of the dying, are so complex that they require expert spiritual and moral guidance to help determine 'what would Jesus do?' or 'what is God's plan in this particular situation?' Connecting a person to an expert for more specific guidance or counseling is part of the E step. We'll talk more about that tomorrow night.

"To sum up, in the V step, you may have the opportunity to share some powerful, life-giving visions and values—in your own words—as they apply specifically to each person and issue. Use what you have learned through the Listening and Learning Wheels and in the O step to guide you.

As Mary Elizabeth looked out at the class, she could see they were touched, but perhaps feeling a little unsure. Sharing the V step presents a powerful opportunity to make a difference in someone else's life, and she wanted to encourage them.

"You can do this! I know, because I have heard so many stories of ordinary people, people just like us, who have used

The L.O.V.E. Approach with life-changing results. Pray to the Lord for insights and wisdom in what to share in this crucial V step. It is very personalized.

"Allow the love of God to flow through you. Remember what we learned on the first night of class. Your relationship with God is key. If you are filled up with His love, it will flow out to other people. You will be His hands, His arms around someone who is in need of love, vision, hope, and support!

"We have covered so much, and there's a lot to be absorbed," Mary Elizabeth said, as she prompted the class to turn to the "What About Me?" section in their notebooks and begin to reflect on what they had learned and how it applied to them personally.

She allowed them to work for a while, digging deep into their own thoughts and feelings, and then announced the well-deserved break.

———————

Mary Elizabeth knew that this section of the training always generated uncertainty for some in the group, and she wanted to respond to as many questions, concerns, and observations as possible before she invited Dr. Meyer to join them to continue his story.

Not surprisingly, Josh raised his hand first. "I've been called a 'Bible-thumper.' I know chapter and verse—memorized lots of the Bible as a kid. It's my comfort zone. If someone tells me a problem, I just lay it on 'em. I'm only trying to share What Would Jesus Do. But people often shut down after that. I realize now that they don't hear me separating the sin from the sinner. I want to do it more like The L.O.V.E. Approach—if I get the chance." Josh hoped that time would come soon—the distance between him and his son was painful.

After several other students commented, Katy spoke up. If she made a public commitment, she thought, she would be more likely to follow through with her intention.

"I've tried to BE Christ for the women in my parish ministry group. But I've stopped short of sharing Christ using words, like the words in the V step. I was afraid the women would think I had an agenda. Plus, I'm not an expert—either in their problems or in sharing the Gospel. So I never said much at all. I was leaving almost everything to the 'experts'! Now I know that God is opening doors for me to speak up in love, share a new vision, and leave the rest to Him."

Mary Elizabeth thanked all those who shared for their honesty. Then she turned the podium over to Dr. Meyer.

"My sharing will be brief tonight because I want you to have plenty of time to share the V step with your partner and small group. I am moved by your vulnerability as you grapple with the challenges of this step, and by the courage I just heard you express—the courage to try it. It's the courage to be involved at a very personal level, sharing the Good News with others who are in such need of the message of hope today.

"How did Coach use this step with me? Well, he kind of wove it into every conversation—into every other step of The L.O.V.E. Approach. From our first meeting, he never left me without some words of encouragement and affirmation. He gently reminded me that I was not a total failure as a husband or as a counselor. I was not stupid; I hadn't wasted my education. I did have options; I could make changes; I was not alone. If I needed more or different training, I had done it before, and I could do it again.

"I'm a believer, so I knew that deep down, even in my darkest moments, God loved me and had created me for a purpose. I remember one conversation when Coach reminded me of that. I was struggling with my faith. He said God gives me all the grace I need; I just have to call on Him. Coach said one of his favorite promises was 'Ask, and you will receive, seek, and you will find, knock, and it will be given to you.' I needed to hear those words again, and at that very moment.

"One vision Coach shared really stuck with me. About my wife. Without being 'preachy,' he reminded me that God joined us as a couple in marriage. This was a chance to live out what it means to be one. I needed to allow her to be my partner— through all the options, the plan, and its implementation. And we needed to include God in everything. A rope of three strands cannot be broken.

"The V step in The L.O.V.E. Approach is crucial. God will provide YOU with the grace to know just when to share new vision and value. And He will even give you the words! I'll pray for each and every one of you. And I'll be back tomorrow night to finish my story."

Michael and Josh, Katy, and Mariana turned their chairs toward one another for the final exercise. They were eager to pick up where they left off in their problem solving with their partners.

They had woven some encouragement and affirmation into their conversations already, in the L and O steps. But was there any deeper vision—about self, God, God's plan, or the specific options or issues—that God was leading them to share with each other?

As they worked in pairs, it was clear that they were deeply engaged in sharing new visions with each other.

When our four moved their chairs closely together in their small group, Katy became the center of their attention. She confided that her women's ministry group was meeting the very next morning, and she had an intuition that God was preparing her to share a new vision and value with someone in the group who was deeply wounded.

They affirmed her loving and gentle heart and her desire to be used more by the Lord, and they encouraged her to speak up when she felt the urging of the Holy Spirit. Finally, they bowed their heads, and each one asked God to give Katy all the grace she needed the next morning.

CHAPTER TEN

TOOLS FOR THE V STEP

When they had finished breakfast, Jesus said to Simon Peter,
"Simon, son of John, do you love Me more than these?"
He said to Him, "Yes, Lord; You know that I love You."
He said to him, "Feed my lambs."

JOHN 21:15

WHAT ABOUT ME?

Reflect on the Bible verse above. Have I ever thought of people I am in relationship with as Jesus' sheep or lambs? How does this change my perspective on these people?

Have I ever thought of myself as feeding or tending Jesus' sheep or lambs—for Him or in His place (that is, being His hands)? What are my thoughts and feelings about this role?

REFLECTION

(Share your answers with your partner or small group)

Do I or did I ever have a person in my life who was an encourager or affirmer? If so, give one or more examples of how this person encouraged or affirmed me, perhaps when I needed it most. How has this influenced me?

Am I an encourager, an affirmer? If so, write down one or more examples of when I have encouraged or affirmed another person. How did the other person respond to my encouragement or affirmation?

If you don't remember taking on this role with another person, is this something you want to do? Or if you have taken on this role before, do you want to do it more often?

If so, name one or more people who might welcome you to be an encourager in their lives and describe what kind of encouragement they need or what you can affirm about each person.

1.

2.

3.

Have I ever taken the opportunity to share a new vision about self, God, or God's plan with another person who is hurting, perhaps feeling lonely, worthless, or unloved? If so, briefly write about that experience. How did it affect the person I shared with? How did it affect me?

What did I learn from that experience? Would I do things the same or differently the next time I have the opportunity?

Who are the people in my life right now who could benefit from a new vision about self, God, or God's plan? Name one or more people and the new vision that they could perhaps see.

1.

2.

3.

Is there anything holding me back from sharing a new vision and value, either in general or with a specific person or persons?

Did I relate to either Josh or Katy as they shared their hesitations in our story? In what ways?

Pray for an opportunity to share a new vision with one or more of the people whose names you wrote down. When you have shared a new vision or value, come back to this workbook and write down the experience and how it affected the other person and yourself.

PRACTICE

Go back to the issues that have been the focus of your sharing with your partner and small group. You have practiced using the L and O steps with your partner. Now practice the V step with each other. What does your partner need most now: encouragement or affirmation, a new vision of self, a new vision of God, or a new vision of God's plan on specific issues, problems, or options?

REFLECTION
(Share your answers with your partner or small group)

What is my response to having my partner share a new vision and value with me?

What was it like sharing a new vision and value with my partner?

CHAPTER 11

———➤●◄———

KATY TRIES THE V STEP

Katy woke up earlier than usual the next morning. She was sure God had given her this extra time to pray for the women's ministry group meeting before she had to go into hyper drive to get the children ready to be dropped off at another mom's home.

She sensed there would be an opportunity this morning to respond more fully to someone in the women's group who was hurting and needed a message of hope. This time she would not withdraw because she was so deep into the emotions being shared. Or because, not being an expert, she might do more harm than good. Or because she might get pulled in over her head. Or because the problems were too complex and might have no solutions at all. She could feel the prayers and remembered the encouragement from Michael, Mariana, and Josh.

When Katy signed up for the women's group, she thought it would be her relaxing morning for spiritual refreshment. She could take advantage of the parish baby-sitting co-op. There was a women's study program on the dignity of women, with videos, workbooks, and a leader's guide. It seemed doable when the pastor asked her to lead the group.

Katy never expected all the underlying issues and problems the women were facing. They surfaced at almost every meeting. She felt helpless. She was ready to quit—until she discovered The L.O.V.E. Approach. Her pastor had been so wise to send her to the training.

That morning the five women gathered at 9:00 a.m. in one of the church's meeting rooms. Besides Katy, a stay-at-home mother of small children, there was a divorced woman with grown children and a very stressful job, a young nurse who was married and had suffered several miscarriages, a widow whose husband had died after a long struggle with cancer, and Ann, a quiet single woman, a sophomore at the university, with very sad eyes. She was still a mystery to Katy.

Their stories, touched upon in almost every sharing, had broken Katy's heart. Shattered dreams and relationships, past and current traumas, loneliness and searching. The women had built up walls and barriers for protection. They were holding on to things that had not been forgiven. Some wondered how a loving God could have allowed certain things to happen.

There were, no doubt, many things they were not sharing that were also causing shame and distress. Yet all these women were here seeking, at the very least, understanding and companionship—and perhaps hope and healing.

Katy opened the meeting with a prayer, then led the group in the lesson for the day, on women's gift of motherhood. The lesson used the term "spiritual motherhood" for those who were not blessed with biological or adopted children but who took other people into their maternal care.

Ann was especially quiet. Katy noticed it was difficult making eye contact with her. She found Ann glancing up at her occasionally, then quickly looking away. She fidgeted in her chair as she wrote reflections in her workbook. Was she so young that she hadn't thought much about the topic? Was the terminology hard to grasp? Was she just tired that morning? Was it too much caffeine?

Any of these explanations might have let Katy "off the hook." But she sensed something else was going on and felt a nudge in her spirit. She should offer to talk more with Ann after the meeting. She prayed that she was ready.

As the group said their concluding prayer and the women were leaving, Katy made a quiet overture to Ann.

"My childcare is good for another hour. Would you have time to stay a bit and talk? I noticed you were a little uncomfortable today. Maybe I can do something, as group leader, to help you feel more comfortable?"

Ann had been looking down, but when she raised her eyes, the look on Katy's face showed deep caring. Katy was always so kind in the group, never judgmental, always accepting, Ann thought. But could she be vulnerable with Katy? Ann felt so confused. But she knew she wanted someone to talk to.

She responded tentatively. "I guess I could stay, but just for a little while—I have class." Ann left herself an "out" if she decided she needed to leave.

She and Katy took more comfortable chairs beside the window. With a welcoming smile, Katy leaned in closer to Ann.

"You know something about me already, from what I shared on the first day—my crazy life as a stay-at-home mom, a little about my marriage and faith journey. I'm so glad you're in the group. I'd love to know more about your story." She waited patiently, continuing to look into Ann's face.

Katy's manner was so gentle and encouraging. Ann concluded that she could trust Katy—even with her darkest secret.

Ann's eyes welled up as she began. She took a deep breath and finally blurted out, "I keep pretending to be someone I'm not. I'm a fake. I go to church, but I can't live with what the Church teaches. I signed up for this women's study to prove I am a woman like you all are, but maybe I'm not. I'm so confused."

Katy reached into her purse, as Ann paused, and handed her a tissue. This sounded "heavier" than Katy expected. She really didn't know what to say.

Then she remembered that times like this is when The L.O.V.E. Approach is most helpful. All she had to do first was just listen. "Please tell me more," said Katy, using her most encouraging voice.

With Katy's nudging—through gentle questions, nods, and caring eye contact—details spilled out.

A couple of months ago, a female friend at college told Ann that she "loved" her. Ann was repulsed at first, but then she couldn't get this girl out of her mind. "She's one of the most beautiful girls on campus—not plain like me," said Ann. "She's texting me revealing pictures of herself, and she wants to meet up, just the two of us." Ann shared that maybe this explains everything—why she wasn't attractive to guys in high school, why they only related to her as someone to hang out with, to shoot baskets with.

Ann told Katy she had been raised in a family with only brothers. She competed with them in everything. Ann never felt close to her mother or her father. There were some other things in the family, she said, things she couldn't talk about.

When she was eleven years old, Ann's mother told her she was a disappointment—she didn't dress and act like the little girl her mother always wanted.

One of her courses at the university covered "gender fluidity." Ann said she felt confused about her "identity." She felt different, lonely, guilty about her attractiveness, her attractions, and her lack of attractions. She felt pressure to "declare her identity"—gay, straight, trans, other. . . . She concluded by saying sadly, "Maybe I'm not a woman like the rest of you in the group."

Katy had avoided expressing shock at Ann's story because her primary feeling was deep sadness. She had the sympathetic feelings that often came over her when she heard stories about how wounded and confused some people are.

But this time she didn't let her feelings overcome her. It was clear that Ann was reaching out for help. Katy was in the right place at the right time. It was a divine appointment. She had prayed for this opportunity. She couldn't help but feel intimidated by the complexity of this situation, but she was committed to forming a relationship with Ann.

Katy guessed that Ann was thinking of either/or options—either stay miserable or succumb to the overtures of the student who was pursuing her with texts and pictures. Ann was probably not thinking of a third option—a path that would involve healing from her woundedness (caused by family issues and perhaps others issues that Ann did not yet want to reveal) and exploring more deeply the true nature of her femininity.

Katy sensed that it was not the time or place to draw an options tree and come to a conclusion based on the pros and cons of Ann's potential choices. Her feelings were too intense right now, and Katy remembered Mary Elizabeth saying that an option chosen at this point generally does not lead to a satisfactory resolution of the problem in the long run.

She decided that she would touch on options only lightly that day. What Ann needed most now was encouragement, a new vision and value, and especially an affirmation of her worth and God's love and plan for her—the V Step.

Katy continued looking into Ann's eyes. "Ann, God has a plan for you. His plans are always for us to prosper, to give us a future and a hope. I would love to talk to you—in depth—about all the potential choices you have. But I think that discussion would best come later, as we continue our relationship and have more time.

"What I want to assure you of right now is that your true identity is not based on a label that you or anyone else places on you! This is far from who you are! God designed you as a special and unique person—your body, soul, and personhood are all woven together. He created you in His own image and likeness.

"When I was a young woman, I had doubts and questions about myself too. Someone shared with me that 'God does not make junk.' It rang true and has helped me ever since with my own self-doubts.

"God designed you for good. It is never God's plan for you to become an object for anyone else's pleasure or to be used as a means to an end. He wants you to be in healthy relationships where you are cherished and loved for who you are as a whole person.

"And God does not want you to be confused about how and why He made you. There is so much misunderstanding today about what it means that God 'created us male and female.' There are outright lies out there too. I know you're hearing very strange things in school. And you're probably dealing with confusing things, even from your childhood, related to your sexuality.

"You made a very smart decision to come to our women's group—to explore how God created us and what He calls us to as women. You are in exactly the right place to find the answers you are searching for!

"I know God guided you here. See how He cares for you? See how he is trying to show you the plans He has for you? Even when you are feeling distant from Him, He is close to you because He loves you so much!

"Here's why I'm sure of that. God has been prompting me too. He was nudging me. That's why I asked you if you wanted to stay after the meeting today. He provided the opportunity for me to reach out to you today because He loves you! It just amazes me how he shows His goodness!"

Ann nodded her head and glanced up occasionally as she listened to Katy, and her body finally seemed to relax as she leaned forward in her chair. A slight smile had formed on her face by the time Katy finished sharing.

"Thank you," Ann said simply. "I do feel a little better—more hopeful just being here now."

"I feel honored," Katy responded, "that you've trusted me with what's on your heart. I want you to know that there ARE good options. You do not have to live with all this internal conflict. And you don't have to give in to the pressures coming from this girl and our culture. You can be the person God created you to be.

"I would love to help you sort through all this, but I'm not an expert in what you experienced in your home and what you are experiencing now. I think I know someone who is, though. Her name is Mary Elizabeth. I trust her. Could I share just the basics of your story, keeping the details confidential, and see what resources and help she suggests?"

Ann looked into Katy's eyes, and for the first time during their conversation, her face looked peaceful. "Yes, I would like that very much."

Katy felt relieved but also a little afraid of the challenges that might lie ahead. Even so, she, too, had a sense of peace. God would provide all the grace they needed.

She had the urge to hug Ann but remembered that sometimes people who are sexually wounded can react negatively to physical touch, and she did not want to threaten the new relationship. Instead she gave Ann a warm smile and said, "Let me talk to Mary Elizabeth—I'll see her tonight—and I'll let you know what she suggests as a next step." They exchanged emails.

"May I pray for you too?" Katy asked. Ann nodded, then bowed her head, and Katy led them in a simple prayer.

CHAPTER 12

———⇒●⇐———

CLASS FIVE—THE E STEP
EXTEND AND EMPOWER

Mariana, Katy, Josh, and Michael entered the training room with mixed feelings. They were all eager to finish out the instruction that was proving to be such a help already, but sad to think that their intense experience of using The L.O.V.E. Approach with each other in their small groups of four—so bonding and encouraging—was coming to an end.

Katy had a quick private few minutes with Mary Elizabeth before she joined the other three.

Seeing the big smile on Katy's face, they huddled quickly. Smiles spread to the faces of Katy's team.

Chatter in the room slowly died down. The trainees took their seats and all attention was directed to the slide on the screen:

L = Listen and Learn
O = Open Options
V = Vision and Value
E = Extend and Empower

"You know the drill by now," said Mary Elizabeth. "Before we begin the last step of The L.O.V.E. Approach, would anyone like to share if you have used it since we met last night, especially the V step?"

By the time several of the trainees told their stories, Michael, Mariana, and Josh had quietly convinced Katy that she should share also. Shyly, she stood up.

"I lead a parish women's group. Up until now I thought I would have to become a professional counselor if I wanted to help these women. Now I realize what I need is The L.O.V.E. Approach—especially the V step! This morning I shared a new vision of self and new vision of God and God's plan with one of the women. I know He guided my words—I couldn't have done it on my own! It was a beautiful moment—seeing the change in her face from fear and confusion to hopefulness. But she needs the help of experts. I need to know how to follow up. Thank you all, especially my small group, for giving me the encouragement to get out of my comfort zone and try to make a difference in someone's life."

"I'm happy to hear how helpful your partners and small groups in this class have been," responded Mary Elizabeth. "Our last class tonight is designed to provide the guidance you need, Katy, and what everyone needs to be successful with the final step of The L.O.V.E. Approach." Mary Elizabeth clicked on the next slide:

- Written plan or action steps—who? what? when? where? how?
- Resources and expert help—information, counseling, spiritual guidance, healing, material

> aid, recovery programs, mentoring, medical care, and more
>
> • Follow-up and support as appropriate

"In the E step we help the other person make a specific plan or at least decide on the first few action steps to implement their chosen option. If you are involved in the issue too—an issue in your family, with a friend, in ministry—the two of you will develop a few action steps to move forward with the option you've agreed on.

"Putting these steps down on paper—who is going to do what, when, where, and how, and what the initial resources might be—does not need to be done in a formal way, especially if you're using The L.O.V.E. Approach in your family or with a friend.

"Sometimes, church ministries where people come for help with specific issues or problems have special forms that can be filled out for this purpose, noting who, what, when, where, and how. Then the appropriate follow-up can occur. This is what we do in the E step where I work at the Guadalupe Center.

"When you are not the person equipped or called to provide the next level of help or care, you can generally connect the person you are helping to someone who is. For referrals, start with the people and networks you know and trust—the agencies in our Christian Coalition, your church, friends, colleagues, family—and if they are not able to help, they may be able to refer you to just the right expert or resource.

"We are blessed with many local experts for one-on-one help. Other resources are available online—for information, research, advice, practical help, and ongoing support. With the internet—and that amazing technology right in our hands—our smartphones—specific help is becoming easier and easier to find!

"Once you have referred the person to the expert help he or she needs, you may not continue to be involved. But you can also follow up, as you feel called—you can touch base, listen, introduce additional options, make practical suggestions, provide more encouragement—in short, you can continue The L.O.V.E. Approach as needed!

"Remember the story of the Good Samaritan? Unlike others, the Samaritan did not pass by the man on the road who had been beaten and left for dead. He intervened, got involved. But the Samaritan was not the one who ultimately nursed the man back to health. He had to proceed on his journey, so he took the man to an innkeeper willing to help, left money for the injured man's care, and then checked on the man when he returned. We can all be Good Samaritans."

Mary Elizabeth paused to let the teaching on the E step and the message of the familiar but powerful parable sink in.

"I've invited Dr. Meyer to join us before the break tonight; he'll share the rest of his story, especially how the E step worked in his situation." Smiling, she turned the podium over to him.

"It's good to be back on your last night of training to finish up my story—how The L.O.V.E. Approach changed my life and led me to where I am now, standing before you, as the executive director of Community Social Services and head of our Christian Coalition.

"You recall that Coach really listened when I was in my 'nightmare job.' He helped me sort through what I could do—using some serious Options Trees! He built up my courage and affirmed my skills. He reminded me of my wife's love and our call to be one in our marriage. He reminded me of God's love and His grace when I was at my lowest—and so much more!

"He also helped me plan how to get here from there.

"After I chose the third option—to try to cut back to part time and transition to a job better suited for me, Coach spent a couple of hours with me and my wife to develop an initial plan of action. On a sheet of paper, we started brainstorming. What action steps did we need to move toward that option? What initial resources could we think of? We had lots of things on the list, and then we tried to put them in some kind of order. Three steps seemed the most foundational."

Dr. Meyer began jotting things on the whiteboard, including the three most important initial action steps: getting a handle on finances, finding help with possible new career paths, and relieving some of the stress, plus a list of their initial resources.

Action Steps
1. Research finances
   What: cuts possible? minimum income needed?
   Who—wife and me
   When—immediate, finish in two weeks

2. Research career counseling/testing
   Who—me
   Where—community college, university, online
   When—immediate, finish in three weeks

3. Relieve stress—God's help
   Who—wife and me
      What and When—walk together three
      nights per week, pray nightly

Resources
- Tax files, bank statements, receipts/bills folders, mortgage, house and car values
- Online searches—career/placement testing, training/degree programs/ jobs?
- Coach's friends who changed careers—Coach will introduce via emails
- Pastor for potential support groups, networking
- God/prayer!

Follow-Up
- Meet with Coach

"Coach offered to meet with us whenever we needed him. We met in person one more time, then he skyped with us a couple times. After about two months, we only called Coach when we wanted specific input and advice.

"Our first plan led naturally to the next one. We got on a roll, and before long I had met with some very knowledgeable and helpful people, we had a file folder full of information and resources, and we began to make changes in our lives.

"I eventually cut back my counseling hours and took courses, some of them online, toward a degree in nonprofit management. After three years, with lots of support from my wife, I was able to leave my private counseling practice and take my present position with Community Social Services. The board encouraged me to finish my management degree, which I was able to do a year later, thanks again to my wife's support as well as my team at the ministry.

"I thank the Lord daily for leading us every step of the way, and especially for the people—my wife and Coach—who were His arms around me whenever I felt alone or discouraged. I am so thankful I can 'give back'—through the Christian Coalition.

"Thanks for listening to my story and for learning my favorite life-changing tool, The L.O.V.E. Approach!"

The class gave Dr. Meyer a warm round of applause. He smiled broadly as he looked at the trainees, encouraging each one with his eyes and with friendly nods. He shook hands with Mary Elizabeth before making his way out of the room.

"Now it's time to try the E step with your partner," announced Mary Elizabeth. "When you break into pairs, review what you have been sharing with each other in the L, O, and V steps. I bet you already have plans in the backs of your minds. Now it's time to put some foundational action steps and resources on paper in your notebooks. Get busy, and I will let you know when it is time to break into your groups of four."

There was a steady murmur throughout the room as the class worked in pairs and then groups of four. Mary Elizabeth made the rounds and glanced over shoulders, seeing action plans and lists of resources quickly taking shape.

Soon it was time for stretching and a short break before moving into the final but crucial segment of the training.

———

"Great job on developing your action plans!" said Mary

Elizabeth when the group had reassembled. "You have now moved through all the stages of The L.O.V.E. Approach with your partner. Congratulations on a job well done! Now, how does it feel to have a plan to tackle that personal issue or problem you have been communicating about all week?"

There were nodding of heads and smiles all around, some handshakes, patting one another on the back, a few hugs, and other gestures of thanks between partners and within the small groups. Mary Elizabeth even noticed a few people reaching for tissues.

"We all know that some of you have already started using The L.O.V.E. Approach with someone in your family, workplace, or ministry, and your reports to the class have been very encouraging. Thank you!

"Dr. Meyer knows how much I love his testimony about how these four steps changed his life. But not every case turns out so beautifully, as I'm sure you suspect. Even when we can provide expert follow-up and support, not every person makes such dramatic life changes, not every problem is solved, not every relationship restored.

"Let's think more deeply about what the E Step, Extend and Empower, involves. It's not merely about a plan, resources, and follow-up. *Extend* means to broaden, lengthen, and even deepen the concrete help available, but it implies something else too. We can 'extend' a hand, but sometimes it's not accepted.

"*Empower* means to give power to a person. With specialized resources and support, we provide power to the individual or family. But their own willpower is also needed. Positive options may not be carried out, the new vision may ultimately be rejected, and problems may continue.

"Even with The L.O.V.E. Approach, issues sometimes remain and broken relationships may not be healed, at least to our knowledge. I bet you're not surprised! We live in a fallen world. We're a wounded people. We're under attack from the forces of evil.

"Only God is all powerful! Don't expect that you alone—no matter how well you use The L.O.V.E. Approach or any other tools—will be able to help people, even someone in your own family, circle of friends, or church, to resolve every issue or problem.

"But as Christians we are called to 'walk with' or accompany those who are entrusted to us, to help them along the way, even as we all struggle.

"As we said in our first class, it is God's love that works through us. That is what gives our sometimes feeble efforts the power that can change lives. And even when we don't see the changes we anticipated, that is what gives us hope.

"I want you to turn now to the "What About Me?" section in your notebooks. You'll find the Parable of the Sower and the Seed, as I've also put on the screen."

A sower went out to sow. And as he sowed, some seeds fell beside the path, and the birds came and devoured them. Other seeds fell on the rocky ground, where they had not much soil, and immediately they sprang up, since they had no depth of soil, but when the sun rose, they were scorched, and since they had no root, they withered away. Others fell among the thorns, and the thorns grew up and choked them out. Other seeds fell on the good soil and brought forth grain, some a hundredfold, some sixty, some thirty. (Matthew 13:3–8)

Mary Elizabeth read the words slowly aloud and then continued. "Jesus later explains to his disciples that the different kinds of ground—shallow, rocky, thorny, rich—are like different hearers. Some don't understand it, so the 'evil one' steals it from their hearts. Some receive it, but with no roots it withers away when tribulation comes. Some receive it, but cares of the world and the lure of riches keep the seed from bearing fruit. But some hear and understand it, and it bears fruit and yields a hundred, or sixty, or thirtyfold!

"Not everything depends on you. It would be really prideful to think that it does. Not only is free will crucial, but God has many other sowers on the job too!

"God has commissioned an army of believers who are scattering good seeds, providing water and nutrients, adding to the soil, pulling up weeds, and helping God's seeds to grow. We are only a handful of His instruments in this world. And it is ultimately God Himself who brings forth the fruit."

With those words of encouragement, Mary Elizabeth instructed the class to begin their reflections on the parable in their notebooks and how it relates to their use of the E step or The L.O.V.E. Approach as a whole.

The class worked diligently on their reflections, talked in pairs, and then, as instructed, moved their chairs to form their groups of four.

Michael, Josh, Mariana, and Katy were more eager than ever to share with one another. Relationships had grown over this week of intimate communication, and they were aware that this was their last class.

Katy offered to go first. With a big smile on her face, she began. "God has already shown me that He is in control, not me! When I shared with you earlier about using the V step with the college student in my parish group, I didn't mention that God was already putting the resources in place that she needs. Mary Elizabeth's Guadalupe Center has counselors who can help her with gender confusion—I checked with her at the beginning of class! Because He is making the plan, I don't feel powerless at all. I'm excited to be a part of what He is doing, and I pray He keeps using me as one of His sowers!"

Mariana responded by patting Katy affectionately on the knee. "As always, we are kind of opposites. I was always in the driver's seat—up until now—knocking down the obstacles, sometimes even other people, to get the job done. It's not good, blaming everyone else when things don't work according to your plan. This week I experienced building relationships as a better way to get the job done . . . together.

"In the parable, I was struck by all the seeds that just died . . . because of the rocks and weeds and shallow soil. I'm committed to helping remove obstacles for other people so they have a chance to grow. I need to get closer to God. I want it to be not just me but Him working through me."

Michael offered to go next. He looked a little sheepish. "I realized tonight that getting the 'system' right, following the right process, doesn't guarantee a successful outcome. That kind of thing works most of the time in accounting. But not with my relationship with Christy. Every night of our class, I tried another step of The L.O.V.E. Approach at home. In the back of my mind, I guess I thought that by the end of the week we'd have a great plan. Relationship problems solved!

"But we both need to make a decision to love, every day, maybe many times every day. I'm glad there are lots of other sowers out there—we're both going to need help. I'm convicted that we need to pray together—at least every night before bed—and trust God for the fruit."

Michael finished somewhat abruptly; he could feel himself choking up a bit. Josh patted his shoulder and began, also fighting back emotions.

"Thanks, Michael, for helping me plan action steps to break the ice with my son. I'm committed to try tonight—if he's home. I've had a feeling something big is happening. I've been able to protect him, get him out of trouble, set him on the right path. I've been in control . . . up until now. He was a kid. But I don't know this time. I'm thanking the Lord that it's not all up to me! It's a relief. I need your prayers, but I know the Lord loves him even more than I do."

Mary Elizabeth hated to break into what she could sense were intense conversations, but it was time to conclude the class. She gave the trainees time for group hugs and exchanging emails and phone numbers for those who wanted to stay in touch.

She reminded them to keep their notebooks close—to review and remember what they had learned about themselves, each other, and about how to Listen and Learn, Open Options, introduce new Vision and Value, and Extend and Empower.

Then she ended with a prayer, thanking God for bringing them together and asking Him to bless each of those present as they went back into their homes, neighborhoods, workplaces, and churches. She prayed that they would treasure their relationships, starting with their relationships with Him. She asked Him to give them many opportunities to use the transformational power of The L.O.V.E. Approach.

Mary Elizabeth put a final slide up on the screen:

Reunion
- Six Months from Today
- Same Place and Time
- Refreshments
- Surprises!

While she was stepping down from the podium, the trainees gave Mary Elizabeth an extended and enthusiastic standing ovation.

CHAPTER 13

TOOLS FOR THE E STEP

A sower went out to sow. And as he sowed, some seeds fell beside the path, and the birds came and devoured them. Other seeds fell on the rocky ground, where they had not much soil, and immediately they sprang up, since they had no depth of soil, but when the sun rose, they were scorched, and since they had no root, they withered away. Others fell among the thorns, and the thorns grew up and choked them out. Other seeds fell on the good soil and brought forth grain, some a hundredfold, some sixty, some thirty.

MATTHEW 13:3–8

WHAT ABOUT ME?

What are my thoughts and feelings about what the Parable of the Sower (above) says about my work not only with the E step, but also with The L.O.V.E. Approach as a whole?

Do I think seeing myself as a sower is a good way to think of our roles? Why or why not?

Have I seen in my own experience that God provides many people to sow seeds, plus people to till the ground, add soil and water, provide nutrients, and pull up weeds, but that God alone brings forth the fruit? If so, please explain.

Do I relate to any of the reflections shared by Michael, Mariana, Katy, and Josh in their small group in our story? Which ones, and why?

PRACTICE

Refresh your memory about the L, O, and V steps you have taken to help your partner with their issue or problem identified in chapter 4. Now help your partner develop a plan, using the E step of The L.O.V.E. Approach. Try to identify three foundational action steps and a list of potential resources, and the follow-up or support that will be needed, as in the example shared by Dr. Meyer. Allow your partner to do the same for you.

Write down your own plan here.

Action Steps

Resources

Follow-Up

REFLECTION

(Share your answers with your partner or small group)

What was my experience of helping someone else develop an action plan and list of resources using the E step?

What was my experience of having someone help me develop my action plan and list of resources using this step?

What did I learn from this experience?

CHAPTER 14

JOSH TRIES THE E STEP

Josh's prayer on the way home was answered. His son's car was in the garage. Now he prayed that he would have the opportunity tonight to use The L.O.V.E. Approach with Marcus. And lastly, he prayed that he would use it wisely.

He would start with the L step if Marcus would talk to him, and just focus on that. Josh knew he had been a terrible listener. He typically did all of the talking. He had the charming gift of gab. He could keep one person or an entire crowd enthralled—he could keep them laughing or crying if he wanted to.

His gift had its flip side, though—his weakness. He almost never followed the advice that Bishop Wilson gave on the first night of training—but it made an impact on him when he heard it. "God gave you two ears and one mouth. Use them in that proportion." He intended to do just that.

Marcus was no longer his little boy, hanging on his every word. He had become a young man when Josh wasn't looking. Now he had to transition to a new way of communicating, a new way of trying to be an influencer in his son's life—The L.O.V.E. Approach.

133

Marcus was in his room with the door closed. Josh knocked loudly. He knew Marcus would likely have his earbuds in—a means he used regularly to tune out his dad.

"Hey, son, can you open up? Would you be willing to talk to me? It's important." Marcus did not respond for several minutes. Josh was just about to begin again when Marcus slowly opened the door a little bit.

"What do you want, Dad? I'm tired. It's late. Maybe tomorrow."

This was a good sign. At least he opened the door and took out the earbuds. Josh decided to be honest with his feelings.

"I'm feeling pretty lonely, son. You haven't taken my calls or answered my texts . . ." Josh realized Marcus might think he was being accused. So Josh stopped quickly and rephrased. "I mean, I know I've been busy, even in the evenings this week. I have an uneasy feeling that something may be wrong. It's only the two of us, son. We need to stick together! Can we talk?"

Nothing in response, but Josh was patient. Marcus opened the door further and stepped aside so Josh could enter. Marcus went back to where he was sitting, with his back against the headboard of his bed, legs outstretched.

Josh sat down on at the foot of the bed and looked intently at his son. His legs had gotten so long! His head was bowed . . . no eye contact. He had his arms crossed, a sign that he was not very open at this point. Josh knew he had to be the first to share his own areas of self-awareness, some of his feelings, thoughts, and wants.

"Marcus, I mean it when I said I've been feeling lonely. I know it's my fault—I've been too busy, and when we are together, I do all the talking. It's all about me, my ideas, my plans for you—not about you or what you're thinking and feeling. I'm judging that I'm not a good dad for an eighteen-year-old, like I was for an eight-year-old. But I want to be. I have a lot to learn. Maybe you can help me. At least this is a start. Thanks for opening the door."

Marcus raised his head and uncrossed his arms. *He's opening up more than the door,* thought Josh. *Thank you, Jesus.*

"I really want to listen to you tonight, find out what is going on with you. Maybe I'm wrong, but looking back over the last couple weeks, something seems to be on your mind; something's bothering you. Maybe it's a bunch of stuff hitting at one time—like the ACT coming up, a new girlfriend, the band, the car, your boss at the drive-through. Regular stuff can really add up.

"But if it's something really big—something you've wanted to keep me from finding out—I just want you to know that nothing you could ever say or do could make me stop loving you. You're my son, and I love you no matter what."

Now Marcus was looking straight into his dad's eyes, and his face showed the stress, even the pain of the moment. He hesitated, then blurted out, "Dad, I don't think you want to hear this. . . I don't know what to do. It's me and Chloe. She found out last week that she's pregnant. I'm the father." That's all he could say for a minute or so.

Josh was momentarily in shock. In the back of his mind, he had guessed some major trouble, but not this. Josh had had the father-son talk with Marcus a long time ago. Whenever he could get the message in, Josh always reinforced the fact that God's plan was marriage between one man and one woman and the place for sexual intimacy and children was within marriage.

He had taught his son that it was beautiful and wonderful that way. Marcus had heard it in Sunday school too—their pastor was big on biblical truths. Josh lived out that value as a single father. How could this happen?

But he remembered enough to control himself and not react quickly, judge, blame, shout, or question. This was not the time to share biblical truths. This was the L step. Instead, he said, "Tell me more about it."

Marcus told the story, ending with the fact that Chloe took three home pregnancy tests the previous week and then told Marcus, in tears, that she was pregnant and considering an abortion.

Josh forced himself not to focus on the complex problem he just heard about. He had learned that the most important thing he could do was to listen and find out what was going on inside his son—besides the stress that he could see on his face. "How did you feel what she told you she was pregnant? And what did you think when she said she was considering an abortion?"

Marcus shared that he first felt kind of excited when she told him she was pregnant. He was in love with Chloe, this was their baby, and he felt the responsibility. But when she told him she was considering an abortion, he didn't know what to think or say. He wanted to say he would help her, that they could get through this together, but then he thought, what kind of help could he be? He was only eighteen with a part-time job. She's the one who was pregnant and would have to carry and deliver the baby.

Marcus concluded, "I thought the best thing to say was that I would help her whatever she decided to do. But then she said that I had abandoned her, that I didn't love her. And she hasn't spoken to me since."

By this time Marcus had moved closer to his dad. Josh reached out and gave his son a hug. Marcus said, "Dad, Chloe won't talk to me. I don't believe abortion is right. This is my baby. I love Chloe. But we're only eighteen. What can we do?"

Josh suggested they move to the kitchen table and think through this some more. "Let's look at the options," he said, reaching for the tablet on the kitchen counter. Josh realized at that point that they would probably be engaging in the entire L.O.V.E. Approach. He had committed to the L step, but he had no idea that it would lead to this. He shot up a silent prayer. "Thank you, Lord, for preparing me for such a time as this."

Josh drew out two lines on the tablet, like the branches of a tree, and labeled one *abortion* and the other *keeping the baby*. They added some lines to each option, marking the pros and cons.

For abortion, they had only cons. What seemed like a pro—Marcus and Chloe could continue their lives as before—was not really true, Marcus decided. They could never be "just like before," and maybe they would be worse—and they would always be parents of a baby who would never be born.

For keeping the baby, they had a cons list too—interrupting their goals, especially Chloe's, disappointing her parents and others, obstacles for parenting a child at age eighteen. But there was one big pro—their baby would be born.

Josh remembered the trap of thinking only either/or—either abortion or keeping the baby. He wondered aloud if there were other options. If they ruled out abortion, were there other options they could think of? They eventually changed *keeping the baby* to *continuing the pregnancy*, and then they wrote down *parenting options*. Under that they wrote *single parenting*, *marriage*, and *choosing parents through adoption*.

Josh was amazed at how Marcus was handling the situation. He affirmed his son's fatherly instinct and desire to do the right thing. Josh told him he was proud of him and the way he was facing into this. The V Step was so natural at this point.

He did not want to be the Bible-thumper, but he sensed it was time to remind both of them of the biblical truth about the value of every human life. He reached into his briefcase and brought out his well-worn Bible. "Son, as I think about this new little life right now, it gives a deeper meaning to one of my favorite psalms, Psalm 139. 'You formed my inward parts, You knitted me together in my mother's womb, I praise you, for I am wonderously made. Wonderful are your works!'"

Marcus did not react negatively, so Josh was relieved that he had not been preachy. He also wanted to present a new vision and value that he hoped Marcus shared.

"If you choose life, God will help you and Chloe every step of the way. I don't want to minimize the challenges, but He will not forsake you. Do you believe that too?"

Marcus quietly affirmed his agreement and said, "Dad, I'm so sorry for what I did wrong, but I don't want to do something else that I know is wrong too. I want to tell Chloe how I really feel. I don't want her feeling alone. She needs to know that I'll stand by her. And I need to find out what help we can get."

Marcus got up from the table, walked quickly to his room, came back with his cell phone, and began searching "pregnancy help." He looked over the choices and dialed the number of a 24/7 hotline called Option Line. In seconds, he was talking to a woman with a very kind voice. She asked Marcus for his zip code and informed him that in his area there were pregnancy resource centers, pregnancy help medical clinics, and a residential program, all offering services that could help in their situation, at no cost to them.

Option Line could make an appointment for them the very next day at a nearby pregnancy help medical clinic. The clinic offered a free ultrasound to confirm the pregnancy. That was the first step. Then the clinic could answer any questions they had and explore their alternatives with them. The woman explained that pregnancy resource centers and clinics can provide and link to a variety of resources, depending on the specific needs. Their pregnancy help medical clinic could assist them throughout the pregnancy and even after the baby was born.

Marcus made an appointment for 5:00 p.m. the next afternoon, but he explained that he might have to change it, depending on Chloe. The woman gave him directions to their local clinic and offered her continuing help via phone, live chat, text, and email. She said that if Chloe wanted to call Option Line, a consultant would be more than happy to talk to her too.

Josh smiled as he realized that Marcus had gotten to the E Step entirely on his own and found the experts he needed. He was proud of how his son was stepping up. He hoped he could continue to guide him in the right paths.

The next thing Josh knew, Marcus had Chloe on the phone. He walked back to his room and closed the door gently. Josh began praying for them and for their baby.

CHAPTER 15

REUNION: MICHAEL, MARIANA, KATY, AND JOSH MEET AGAIN

Six months exactly from the first evening that our four met, they came together again in the church hall.

Almost all of the trainees from their class gathered for the reunion and a refresher—talks by Dr. Alex Meyer from Community Christian Services and Mary Elizabeth McDowell of the Guadalupe Center. Bishop Isaiah Wilson from Calvary Bible Church was also there to pray over all the participants and the ministries. He received several rousing "Amens" that evening.

A couple of surprises were included, as Mary Elizabeth had promised. Everyone was happy to meet Dr. Meyer's wife, Sharon, and Coach, who had been so instrumental in Dr. Meyer's journey. Their story was so familiar that they were welcomed practically as family.

The trainees, most leading church ministries or teams, had also been invited to bring a ministry participant, team member, or family member who had a story to share about the impact of The L.O.V.E. Approach.

The young man Josh was mentoring at the King Boys' Ranch touched everyone. He told how Josh shared with him that the Lord had a plan and purpose for his life—and that's what made all the difference.

Michael shared with the group how the St. John Food Pantry board was using The L.O.V.E. Approach. He focused on the way his fellow board members intentionally used the L step at board meetings. It made the board decision making so much more respectful and satisfying. Michael was convinced that it helped them do God's work in a God-honoring way.

When the formal program finished, Michael, Josh, Mariana, and Katy eagerly started to catch up.

They couldn't help talking about the four steps of The L.O.V.E. Approach. It was part of their vocabulary now—and a mention of any of the steps brought smiles.

They kept coming back to Josh's big news. Marcus' girlfriend Chloe was due to deliver a baby girl in less than two months. The L.O.V.E. Approach was helping not only Josh and Marcus, but Chloe and her parents too. Every step was being used again and again—there were so many issues, feelings, thoughts, wants, values, needs, resources, options, and plans still to be made.

Chloe had been adopted as a baby, and the young couple and their families are prayerfully considering that loving, parenting option. Josh shared that Marcus and Chloe were also discerning whether marriage is the Lord's plan for them, and they enrolled in a marriage prep course at Bishop Wilson's church. Either option would be challenging, but they now have so much support—their parents, the church, and all the resources of the pregnancy help organization.

Michael said that he and Christy were so excited about their relationship. It has dramatically changed, thanks especially to the L step. They recently committed to a church-based marriage mentoring program in which a young couple—engaged or married—asks an older couple to meet with them regularly in an accountability group.

Michael also said that he and Christy wanted to meet Marcus and Chloe. They could be part of the mentoring program too. Michael shared that he thinks of Josh as a role model for the kind of father he wants to be—hopefully soon.

Mariana reported that her admin team at the mega church is thriving, and her employee Tomas too. She has become a much better team leader because of her training in The L.O.V.E. Approach. But she also has realized that she wants and needs more spiritual "feeding," and so she has joined Katy's weekly women's ministry group. She said she loves experiencing how Katy uses the V step in her small group.

Mariana shared that she also had been doing informal career coaching with Ann, who has accepted an internship on Mariana's admin team. Amazingly, Tomas invited Ann to join him and a group of young adults from the church on a trip to the championship game this weekend. Her two mentees!

Katy said she knows she's working in her calling and at last feels equipped. The four steps are becoming natural in her ministry and in her family too. She volunteered that she would be available to keep Josh's grandbaby for a few "shifts" when needed, so Chloe can graduate and Marcus can work and continue school. She said her family would love having a baby in their home.

As Mary Elizabeth listened to these success stories, she was grateful that, as her students have continued to use the four steps, their relationships were becoming even stronger. They were making gifts of themselves to others in their lives, and it was beautiful to witness.

———>●<———

The seeds planted when Michael, Josh, Mariana, and Katy learned and experienced The L.O.V.E. Approach together are producing fruit. That fruit is already creating new seeds. Those seeds are being sown and cared for, and God—the Lord of the harvest—will produce even more fruit. The process continues—with eternal impact.

ACKNOWLEDGMENTS

I am grateful to my husband Mike Hartshorn, whose commitment to "dialoguing" (more intimate couple communication) in the early years of our marriage led to my developing the Listening and Learning Wheels and using them to train volunteers in pregnancy help organizations.

Thank you to my dear sister Sally Metzger, also a writer, who has been my best critic and encourager through this process.

Thank you to all who read the text carefully and gave valuable suggestions, in particular members of the Heartbeat International team, present and past, who have been involved in many stages of the writing and production of this book, especially Andrea Trudden, Jennifer Wright, Betty McDowell, Beth Diemert, Mary Peterson, Tim Stephens, Zeke Swift, and Deb Schirtzinger.

Thank you especially to Heartbeat's President Jor-El Godsey, who has prioritized Heartbeat International Publishing and supported, in many ways, my passion to more widely share the four steps of The L.O.V.E. Approach.

Thank you to the highly qualified experts who, despite their busy schedules, read the manuscript and honored me with their endorsements. Finally, I am grateful to my editor, Claudia Volkman, who believed in the book for a long time and finally could put the "finishing touches" on it!

HEARTBEAT INTERNATIONAL

Every woman facing an unintended pregnancy is on a journey toward a life-and-death decision. Wherever she is on her journey, Heartbeat International is here to help. That's the Heartbeat difference.

Since 1971, Heartbeat International has been:

- The first network of pro-life pregnancy help organizations founded in the U.S. and the largest network in the world.
- Strategically providing direction and education for pregnancy help organizations, including pregnancy help medical clinics, pregnancy resource centers, maternity homes, and adoption agencies worldwide.
- Leading the pregnancy help movement and serving over 2,900 affiliate locations on all six inhabited continents to provide life-saving support to those at-risk for abortion.

Heartbeat's Life-Saving Mission is to REACH and RESCUE as many lives as possible, around the world, through an effective network of life-affirming pregnancy help, and to RENEW communities for LIFE.

REACH: Heartbeat Is Always Available for Women in Need

Answering cries for help (in English and Spanish) every hour of every day, Heartbeat's Option Line is the only 24/7 web-based nationwide pregnancy helpline.

OptionLine.org or 1-800-712-HELP (4357)

A life is saved through Heartbeat's network every four minutes. Wherever a woman is on her pregnancy journey, whether she has just discovered she is pregnant, is seriously contemplating abortion, or is seeking information on how to reverse a chemical abortion, our trained consultants answer the call and connect her to the help she needs.

- Option Line provides online scheduling for a seamless connection from Option Line to a local pregnancy center.
- Option Line also answers calls for the Abortion Pill Rescue Network, helping women reverse the effects of taking the Abortion Pill.

Each day, Option Line answers more than 1,100 calls for help by phone, live chat, text, and email, resulting in more than 3.2 million women served since Option Line took its first call in 2003.

RESCUE: Heartbeat Is the Leading Provider of Pregnancy Services

Heartbeat provides the most comprehensive Pregnancy Help Network. Every day, more than 11,000 staff and volunteers open their pregnancy help organizations to meet the needs of those in their communities. Each year, more than 2 million women and men are served in these organizations.

Working with our pregnancy help network, Heartbeat provides:

- Top-notch training and continuous learning opportunities.
- Resources specifically designed for those working in the pregnancy help community.
- Education for more than 6,500 women and men each year online, in person, and on-site.

RENEW: Heartbeat Is Developing Centers in Underserved Locations

Along with rescuing lives at-risk for abortion, a community gains a vital outpost for the culture of life when adding a pregnancy help service location.

The Pregnancy Center Life Launch Grant helps start-up centers open their doors and advance pregnancy help to new communities throughout the U.S. By walking alongside these new centers with training and providing state-of-the-art technology, we share our expertise and expand the pregnancy help community in the most effective way.

We invite you to connect with Heartbeat International and your local pregnancy help organization that is listed in the Worldwide Directory on our website:

www.HeartbeatInternational.org

We also invite you to help spread The L.O.V.E. Approach!

Visit **TheLOVEApproachBook.com** to:

- Download the graphics in the book (Listening and Learning Wheels, a blank Options Tree, important lists like 10 Barriers to Listening, and more). The graphics will help you remember the key concepts, use them in important conversations, and teach others the four steps of The L.O.V.E. Approach.
- Order additional copies of the book.
- Read what others are saying about the book.
- Connect with the publisher.
- Learn more about Heartbeat International.

HEARTBEAT INTERNATIONAL
5000 Arlington Centre Blvd., Ste. 2277
Columbus, Ohio 43220